ELECTRIC DREAMS ROAD TRIP

An Electric Car Adventure

Paul Amess

*For Uncle Mally, who taught me
all about the countryside*

CONTENTS

INTRODUCTION

I had wanted to trace the watershed of England for some years but had never found the time to actually do it. When I say that, I probably mean that I had instead found excuses not to do it. For instance, I couldn't walk it because it was several hundred miles and would take too long, and I simply didn't have the time. When I considered biking it instead, which would solve the time problem, a whole host of other problems reared their ugly head, which I will explain later.

So, when I suggested to my good friend Rob that we embark on a road trip along the watershed of England, he almost spat his beer out and pointed out that we were no longer teenagers and should instead probably stay at home and do something more mature, such as cutting the grass or washing some windows. I say almost spat his beer out, but I should mention that Rob is certainly not one to waste good beer, so after a considerable period of reflection and serious thought, lasting almost four seconds, Rob said that actually, yes, he would probably be up for that.

I had bought my electric car some years earlier,

and it was one of the earliest of its type, being a first-generation Nissan Leaf. I had driven it year-round, from winter to summer and back again and through the changing seasons, and had enjoyed thousands of miles of smooth motoring which had incidentally cost almost nothing, until the previous winter, that is, when something had gone drastically wrong and which almost ended up with the car being taken to a scrapyard and recycled into ashtrays and paperweights, but more of that later.

I had been at university when I made my rather impulsive and not insubstantial purchase, and I fondly remember emptying my bank account of my precious student finance somewhere near the end of 2017 to buy something very expensive from hundreds of miles away that I had never actually seen or driven. I panicked for a day or two, wondering whether I had made the wrong choice, as at the time there were still relatively few electric cars on the road, but my fears evaporated completely the moment a flatbed truck turned up carrying my little blue Nissan.

In no time at all, the driver had dropped the car outside my house and sped off in a cloud of diesel smoke, with some irony, I thought at the time, leaving me alone with my precious new toy. Jumping in, I realised I barely knew how to drive the thing, having only briefly driven one owned by my cousin several months before, but this problem was soon solved through the miracle of the internet and a couple of videos.

The first thing that hit me about driving an electric car was not what I had expected. I had imagined that the main difference would be the lack of petrol or diesel fumes, but considering most modern cars don't smell all that much, this was clearly not the case, and probably never was. The main point to note, in fact, was the smoothness and the lack of vibration when driving electric. My old car, which I had disposed of some months before when I played a game of chicken with a tree, had actually been a pretty nice car to drive, but as I took my first tentative journey around the local area where I lived, I simply could not believe how smooth the ride was compared to my old fossil-fuelled beast. The tree won the game of chicken, by the way, as you would probably expect, and after my little mishap, I did spend some months riding my bike around the city. Still, after noticing that several motorists appeared to be trying to assassinate me, I decided to get another car and go for an electric one at that.

Anyway, I digress. There was no changing gear, of course, as all electric cars are automatic, which meant no finding the biting point of the clutch and not having to worry about when to go from one gear to the other, something which is, of course, the main cause of vibration in a geared car. It was not only smooth, but incredibly quiet too, something which I had in fact anticipated, and for the first few months of scampering around town, I was pretty nervous about becoming a pedestrian assassin myself, but soon found this not to be the case.

At slow speeds, most noise produced by a car comes from the tyres, and this is so regardless of whether your fuel of choice is petrol, electric, or if your name is Marty McFly, plutonium. I found that most people don't rely on just noise alone when deciding whether or not to set foot into a possibly busy road, and some are even clever enough to use their eyes, so I was glad to report that after several months of happy motoring, the kill-count remained firmly at zero.

That all changed one dark and wintry night in December of 2018, however. On that fateful evening, a hoodie-clad young man with earphones in, which were loudly broadcasting the best of Led Zeppelin to anyone within 20 yards, by the way, happened to look down at his phone as he crossed a road near to the university, rather than looking left as he probably should have done.

Had he looked left, he would have seen a big blue thing with wheels and headlights approximately ten feet away from him but certainly moving in his direction. He would have also seen a bloke wearing glasses behind the steering wheel, with his mouth about to develop the shape that pronounces 'F' words, but as he did not look, he saw none of this, bless him.

I had already attempted to put the brake pedal through the bottom of the car, but to cut a long story short, some pesky physics meant that the space occupied by my car and the space occupied by this stranger's body ultimately collided and fought it out for a few seconds. Obviously and perhaps inevitably, there is no way a spotty teenager is ever going to get one over on a ton of metal, and the last thing I remember is seeing said teenager sliding down the very smooth front end of a blue 2011 Nissan Leaf.

I jumped straight out, of course, despite the rain, not knowing what to think about the apparent pile of rags on the floor before me. Was he dead, I wondered, a question which was answered pretty quickly when the pile of rags stood up in front of me. His mouth moved to the same position that mine had recently been in, you know, the one that pronounces 'F' words, but instead, an 'S' word came out, as he apologised profusely to me.

If there is one thing I love about us Brits, it is that we apologise for absolutely anything, whether it is our fault or not. When someone bumps into us, we will actually say sorry to that person, which I have always found odd in itself. But then the person doing the bumping will often do the same, resulting in a competition of sorriness, with both insisting that whatever happened was their fault, and then repeatedly asking the other person if they are okay, and if they are sure they are okay, and even if they are sure that they are sure. I've seen this countless times in my life, and it can be really funny, but not, of course, when you have just run someone over.

Luckily, he wasn't hurt, and after an exchange of pleasantries and several dozen apologies, we both went our separate ways, hopefully never to meet again. I did have a couple more near-misses after this, often involving pedestrians who had apparently, at some point earlier in the day, been involved in an accident with a tube of superglue and a mobile phone, but nothing so dramatic or interesting as that dark, wintry night, thank goodness.

I continued using my little car to commute to and from university and work, and luckily the university had recently installed several charging points, something that my home town was desperately short of at the time, as was much of the rest of the country, in fact. As a double-bonus, the chargers were free, which effectively meant free motoring when you consider that you do not have to pay road tax for electric cars either, with the only expense being the insurance, if you bother with that sort of thing.

It was also while I was at university that I first came across the watershed of England. I had been glancing through one journal or another when I came upon a pretty map of the country, which seemed to split the whole place into several neat and colourful groupings of rivers. They ran like veins, which in a way they sort of were, bringing life to the land with the water they carried, but as I looked at the map, I became aware of the very obvious lines that formed the boundary of each catchment area, which is the actual watershed of course. Almost immediately, I wondered to myself whether or not it would be feasible to follow a route that would, in effect, make it possible to travel all of the way through the heart of England without crossing a bridge.

I spent some time trying to find out whether or not anyone had ever followed this route, and if there was, they had certainly hidden their efforts very well, as my searches initially came up empty. However, after many late nights sat in front of a blue screen, I did finally find someone who appeared to be attempting to travel the full length of the watershed in England, but he had started it in around 2013, was only around halfway through it, and did not appear to be currently active.

Anyway, he was walking it, section by slow section, and I had already decided this would not be practical for me, which is when I had briefly considered following the route by bicycle. I seriously considered this option, even though it would be a mammoth thousand-mile bike ride, confident, initially at least, that I would be able to do it.

However, the first task was to identify the route, and for this, I did it the old-fashioned way. My son had bought me a road atlas for Christmas the previous year, which was bang up to date, apparently. Incidentally, I always wonder how they manage to print the maps off in one year, then market them as being for the following year, but there you go.

Anyway, I looked again at the watershed map and tried to roughly guess where the watershed line might run. Then, I opened my trusty atlas and spent around a week carefully drawing a line that snaked in between the many rivers. I'm sure that there is a high-tech way to do this, but like I said, I'm old school, and anyway, I am glad to report that the line I ultimately ended up drawing by hand turned out to be pretty accurate, as I later found a map on the internet that could have saved me a lot of time, it has to be said.

My route, then, would take me from just to the west of Portsmouth up towards Basingstoke before turning west towards Devizes. Turning north again, the path would snake its way between Swindon and Cheltenham and then head northeast towards and passing Banbury before doing an almost perfect circle around Coventry, which is quite fitting though I will explain why later. The outskirts of Birmingham would then launch us north once again, initially straight through Wolverhampton before passing west of Stoke. The delightful Peak District would lead us between Holmfirth and Manchester, a direction which would take us next into my beloved Yorkshire. Following a path between Burnley and Skipton, the beautiful Yorkshire Dales would be next, passing close to places such as Settle, Garsdale and Hawes, all lovely places in their own right. Continuing north, the route would pass close to Kirkby Stephen and Haltwhistle, leading us into the fantastic forests of Northumberland, before finally finishing close to Kielder on the Scottish border.

It seemed pretty simple, then, that all we had to do was to follow the roads closest to the line of the watershed, and we could, in theory, travel through the whole of England without crossing a bridge.

Earlier, when I was still considering biking the route, the plan seemed simple and straightforward. A train would take us first to Portsmouth, where we could begin our little bike ride, and when we had finished, we could bike back to Haltwhistle or Hexham and get the train home. As I said, simple and straightforward, or at least it seemed.

Now, if you have ever tried to book a train ticket that included a bike, you may already be aware of some of the pitfalls involved. First of all, there is the size of your bike to consider. If you happen to be a clown by trade and wish to take your unicycle on your daily commute, then that is great, and you do not require a reservation. However, if you want to take anything bigger than this, then good luck to you. Depending on which train company you are using, you either do, do not, or might possibly need a reservation for your bike. Now, I am not sure about you, but when I am booking a train ticket, the last thing I am aware of is generally the name of whichever company will be taking me from A to B, because I simply don't care. I just want to get from A to B as quickly and safely, and cheaply as possible, and in this case, preferably with my bike.

As you might imagine, if you are going from one part of the country to another, you may also be using more than one train company, as they tend to operate in specific areas only, which means, once again, that you will need several reservations, even if you are taking only one bike. Or you might not, but again, good luck with figuring that out.

Next is the timing of the trains. Suppose you plan to do a long journey, such as one to Portsmouth from where I live. In that case, you might want to set off rather early so as to arrive at a reasonable time because that would make sense, wouldn't it? The problem with this is that some train companies, again only some, although which ones who knows, will not let you take a bike on a train during peak hours. What are the peak hours? Well, again that depends on which train company you are travelling with, if you know who they are, of course, which you probably don't. Generally, though, peak hours are before 10am and after 4pm. Unfortunately, the journey I wanted to take is 7 hours long, so can you see the problem with completing it between 10am and 4pm because I certainly can.

Suppose, by some minor miracle, you manage to find a train company that will let you take your bike when you wish, and on the journey you desire. In that case, you will still need some good luck, as there are generally only a handful of bikes allowed on any particular train. However, you cannot book your bike space at the same time as you buy your ticket, because that would just be silly, wouldn't it? Instead, you must buy your ticket and then ring them, which raises the possibility of buying a train ticket that could be useless if they decline your request.

And suppose by yet another miracle, you have managed to sort all of this out and actually get to the point of the journey itself. In that case, you still need to find the specific carriage where you can put your bike, for which the train companies suggest you turn up a few days early at the station and maybe ask some of the staff or a friendly homeless person because when I asked, nobody knew.

I tried this process online and did not do well, so when I rang instead, I was already in a state of deep despair and confusion. Unfortunately, this confused state was compounded further by the lady at the other end of the line. In retrospect, I think she was playing with me in the manner that a cat would play with a dead mouse. For instance, I could not travel early because my local train company operated the 10am rule, and I could not go via London, the most direct route, because bikes were not allowed there, apparently. Instead, she said, I would have to travel via Cardiff or Copenhagen or some other obscure place, off-peak on the second Sunday of last month, if I wanted to have any chance of getting there any time before the next ice-age destroyed the planet and killed us all. Furthermore, she told me I would have to change at Bishop's Itchington or Sandy Balls, which I suspect were names she made up simply to test my patience.

Finally, she advised me that the cost for this journey would be a thousand pounds plus my right kidney, which is kind of the point where I gave up on the idea of riding a bike up the middle of England. To be honest, I don't think I would have had any chance of finishing it anyway, as I have not ridden a bike any distance for around twenty years.

This was when my thoughts turned to driving my little electric car along this route instead. It would make the journey a lot quicker, keeping my better half happy with the fact that I would only abandon her and the children for a few days, as opposed to a few weeks, and driving a car is about the level of activity that my flabby old form can manage, as opposed to riding a heavily laden bicycle for a thousand miles or so. The only issue, however, was with the car itself. As I may have already mentioned, it is a first-generation model and is several years old. Now, the thing with electric cars is that as they get older, their batteries deteriorate, and mine was now ten years old, give or take.

Even in the few years I have had it, I have definitely noticed the range decreasing, but this has not been a problem when using it as a city car and charging it at home every night. When I bought it, the garage explained to me that a battery's state of health is measured in bars and that a healthy battery shows twelve bars, but mine only had eleven at the time of purchase. I bought it anyway because I'm just crazy like that, but to cut a long story short, after almost sixty thousand miles, my little Leaf's battery was now down to nine bars, which effectively meant that it had lost approximately one-quarter of its capacity, which had only been around 84 miles when brand new.

This obviously translates into less range regardless of how you look at it, but whenever people ask me how many miles I get to a charge, I have to explain that it is very difficult to say, as so many factors can affect the range. The temperature is the obvious factor. Additionally, whether it is raining, how windy it is, and things such as how fat the driver or passengers are or how much crap you have left in the boot all have an impact. However, if pushed, I would say that this car will currently take me around fifty or perhaps sixty miles, but even that is not the end of the story. Yes, the car could, in theory, travel fifty miles, but what if you get to your destination and the charger you had intended to use is either out of order, already occupied, or has recently been hit by a meteorite? Well, whatever eventuality you pick means that you are not charging there, so you must also have a backup plan, which is a problem if you only have two miles of range left and the next-nearest charger is ten miles away at Titty Ho in Northamptonshire. And before you ask, yes, that is a real place and is one of the reasons I love this country.

Anyway, this means that you must plan and prepare for any journey and have options available if you run into any problems. For me, that meant joining a breakdown service and storing a gallon of water in the boot along with a catering sized box of snickers bars, just in case. We might run out of electricity, but at least we wouldn't starve to death.

HEADING SOUTH

For anyone who has seen the episode of Only Fools and Horses called *To Hull and Back*, you might think you have some idea of how remote my little home city is. Well, I'm afraid you are wrong. We are literally at the back of beyond. The train stops here and goes no further, not that there is anywhere to go really, and the motorway doesn't even get here, never mind stop here. The only thing past Hull is the North Sea, and I've heard it said that the Yorkshire coast is the fastest eroding one in Europe, possibly the world. This means that the sea, at least, is getting closer to the town every year, but to be honest, this should be seen as a positive, as everyone likes a day out at the seaside.

Anyway, it was a bright and sunny Tuesday morning when I picked Rob up from his house, stuffed his luggage into the boot and the back seat, and we set off on the long drive south towards Portsmouth. I had no idea how long the journey would take, but we were going to be over-cautious and stop for a charge at every opportunity to keep that battery topped up nicely. Rob's wife had made a sign for us to put in the car window, and I was amused to find that it read *grumpy old men on tour*, which described us pretty well, I thought, and after putting it in pride of place, we were off. We soon left the city via the back roads, and the first obstacle was the formidable Humber Bridge, which would take us south into North Lincolnshire.

The plan was to follow the minor roads wherever possible, and there was a method in this madness. The slower you go, you see, the further your range. If we flew down the motorway at seventy, we would get fewer miles out of the battery, but if we tootled along on minor roads, we should get a bit more, at least in theory. So, once across the bridge, I pulled off the dual carriageway at the earliest opportunity, and we headed cross country towards Brigg. Lincoln was our first destination as such, at a little over sixty miles away, so I thought it prudent to get a quick top-up charge in between, and Brigg offered just this.

On the way to the town, though, we realised one other unexpected benefit of following the minor roads. They were so enjoyable to drive along. We were not going very fast, probably somewhere between forty and fifty, because the road was very hilly with lots of tight turns. But we found ourselves enjoying the views immensely as we drove through woods and along farmers' fields with scarecrows and sheep and cows to keep us entertained along the way.

I mentioned to Rob that this was how people

travelled before someone decided that it would be a good idea to build motorways and bridges and bypasses everywhere, and to be honest, other than the time saved, I think the motorways and by-passes have spoilt motoring completely. What we were doing was just such an enjoyable ride, and as we pulled into Brigg, we couldn't believe that an hour had passed as we had been enjoying ourselves that much, and it had felt like just a few minutes.

Our charging point was at a supermarket, in this case, Tesco. The company had recently invested a fair bit of cash in electric chargers, something I discovered when I visited my local branch a couple of months prior and found four gleaming chargers all ready to go. There are many different types of chargers, and some are free while others must be paid for, and generally, the rapid chargers cost you money. On this trip, when I had been looking at the locations of various chargers, I had tried to find free ones as much as possible, figuring that we could take a walk around the local area while we waited for the car to charge up, which is exactly what we did in Brigg.

I had never really been to this small little market town before, and while there was not a lot here, it was a pleasant enough place. We only needed to wait for thirty or forty minutes here, as that would give the car enough charge to get us on to Lincoln, and this proved to be just the right amount of time to wander around the compact but very nice town centre.

In no time at all, or so it seemed, we had enjoyed our little walk, unplugged the car, and were once again on our merry way, following the minor roads but now headed for Lincoln. The car told us that it had 44 miles of range left, and as it was only around 30 miles or so to Lincoln, we trundled along quite happily. Once again, the roads twisted and turned through some pretty villages for a few miles before dumping us onto an old Roman road that headed for Lincoln in a dead straight line, which was clearly the shortest way to the town. At one point, the satnav told us to turn off, although why it did so was beyond us, so being stubborn old men who knew best, we just ignored it.

Unfortunately, after a few miles, we encountered a policeman at a roundabout who had closed the road ahead for some unknown reason. He shook his head at us as if he was addressing little children, which he basically was, and pointed us on our way. Not knowing the next quickest route, we now decided to follow the satnav in the car after all, gritting our teeth about the extra miles we would now have to cover and wishing we had done as we were told the first time.

It is important to state, once again, that an electric car does not have a set range and that several factors can affect this. One factor we were now encountering was hills, and as we slowly followed the other diverted cars up a rather steep one, the range displayed on the dashboard dropped dramatically. I decided that I was now going to call it the guessometer, as it seemed to me that the car was simply guessing how much range was left, and I also decided that I no longer trusted that devious little device after all.

The miles left on the car seemed to drop quicker than the miles left to Lincoln, and as we pulled into the town, the figures were almost neck and neck. I pondered whether or not another diversion would mean we would not make it and prayed that there were no more problems. There is actually a name for this phenomenon, and that is range anxiety. Basically, it is the worry that you will run out of fuel before you get to your destination, and I can tell you firmly that it is real.

Luckily for us, as the battery depletes, the range seems to become more accurate. Perhaps the engineers did this deliberately, as the last few miles suggested that we would, in fact, get to our destination without running out of electricity, but it was certainly a close call. I had heard that when one of these cars is almost out of fuel, a little tortoise appears on the dash board and the car is restricted to a very low speed to conserve energy but will at least allow you to get off whatever busy road you are on so you don't get squashed by a truck. I had not yet witnessed this myself, and I certainly did not want to do so today.

We were lucky, as, with only five miles left on the car, we finally got to our destination, which was another Tesco supermarket. We drove slowly around the vast car park until we found the chargers, which were right at the other side, of course, but then looked in shock to find them all occupied. This was a disaster, as we did not have enough range to get to the next nearest charger, and we could not simply sit and wait as these car parks restrict the time you can spend in them, in this case to three hours.

The gods were shining on us, though, because one of the cars occupying a charger drove away just as we pulled up, although I ended up at the wrong side of the charger. However, our happiness was short-lived as an elderly gentleman waiting for his car to charge told us that the now-empty charger appeared to have problems. After a brief chat, I asked him to stand in the bay for me while I brought my car around and figured we would try it anyway.

The way chargers operate is different from one to the next. There are many companies operating chargers, and most have apps for your phone should you wish to use them, which can be a bit confusing. Some don't have apps at all, and you can just pay with your credit card, while some are simply plug and play, though these are rare. The Tesco chargers are all part of the Pod Point network, and these are generally pretty simple to operate. When you plug your car in, it will begin charging immediately. You then have fifteen minutes to access the app to confirm the charge, which will allow you to charge for longer than the initial fifteen minutes. However, if you forget to confirm the charge, it will stop charging after fifteen minutes, and when you come back to your car, you will have to start all over again and will, of course, have a very long wait. I have done this myself and don't plan on doing it again, ever.

The signs were good anyway. I plugged the Leaf in and heard the confirmation beep from the car that signalled the start of a charge, and then I went onto the app and confirmed the charge. Once I had done this, we stood talking to the gentlemen for a while about cars and chargers, as us men tend to do, and he was very pleasant. He was driving a much newer car, and when he told me that it had a range of two hundred miles, I must admit I was a bit jealous. We explained what we were doing, and I guess he thought us mad or stupid, or possibly both, judging by his laugh. Nonetheless, he wished us luck, but as he drove off, I saw that he was still laughing at us, which made me wonder if we were, in fact, mad or stupid, or possibly both.

We had three hours to kill then, and incidentally, that is how long the car was telling us it would take to charge fully. Luckily, there is probably no finer city to be stuck in for three hours than Lincoln, so we headed up a steep hill towards the city centre to look around the place on possibly one of the hottest days of the year.

I have been to Lincoln many times, being close to my home as it is, but I had not been for approximately eighteen months for the same reason that many people have not been anywhere for eighteen months, which was, of course, the pandemic. Boris had only announced the relaxation of measures yesterday, which is exactly why we were setting off today.

I suspected not a lot would have changed, and I was right. The cathedral and castle were exactly where I had last seen them, as you would expect, I guess, and there were still tourists on every street corner, though fewer in number, looking up in awe and taking photos of everything they could see. I hear that the Cathedral has been particularly popular after standing in for Westminster Abbey in the movie *The Da Vinci Code* after the filmmakers were refused permission to use the actual abbey itself. The castle is popular too, partly because it was built by William the Conqueror, who was really, really good at building castles, it has to be said, but also because it is one of the few places where you can grab a glimpse of the Magna Carta, but it too has been a film star, with parts of it being used in the incredibly popular *Downton Abbey*, in this case for the prison cells.

As for the cathedral, it had actually been the world's tallest building for a couple of hundred years, which is pretty amazing when you think about it. At 524 feet high, the central spire was built around 1300 and remained the tallest structure in the world until it was superseded by St Mary's Church in Stralsund, Germany, which was 495 feet high. I imagine you are wondering how a smaller church became the world's tallest building? Well, this is because the spire at Lincoln spectacularly collapsed in 1549, which must have been an amazing sight, it has to be said. The modern tower is only 272 feet high, and as I looked up at it today, I found it amazing that there was once a spire here that stood almost as twice as tall as what was before me now. No wonder it collapsed, I thought to myself.

Interestingly, the spire that had stood in Lincoln remained the tallest structure the world had ever seen right up until December 1884, which is when those industrious Americans placed the cap atop the Washington Monument along with its aluminium tip, bringing it to a height of 555 feet, which is of course 31 feet higher than Lincoln Cathedral had previously been. The monument did not retain its top spot for long, however. Gustave Eiffel started work on his now-famous tower in Paris in 1887, and within just a couple of years, the structure was completed. This is pretty amazing when you consider that it had taken almost forty years to build the Washington Monument, twenty years to build Lincoln Cathedral and a similar time to build the Great Pyramid, which had previously stood as the world's tallest structure for an estimated 3,000 years.

Since then, many skyscrapers have pushed the record up, literally, and the title for the world's tallest building has changed hands no less than nine times in the last century, but this trend will probably not continue. It is said that the optimum height for a skyscraper is sixty-three floors, as, above this point, it can become uneconomical to continue, but this is obviously an arbitrary limit. The current record holder is the Burj Khalifa, completed in 2008. It resembles a huge upside-down icicle and is an incredible 2,717 feet tall, or about ten Lincoln Cathedrals.

Several other projects have been suggested and even started, but all have failed to deliver. Perhaps most prominent among the wannabees is the Jeddah Tower in Saudia Arabia, with construction started in 2013 but now stalled because the person paying for it, Bakr bin Laden, is currently languishing in a prison cell. Whether this is a good thing or not, I do not know, but it would have been very ironic indeed if the half-brother of Osama bin Laden had actually gone on to build the tallest building in the world, wouldn't it?

Anyway, back to Lincoln. We wandered around admiring almost everything we saw because Lincoln really is that nice, and after a couple of extremely hot and sticky hours, we returned with achy necks back to the car. It was more or less fully charged, and as we pondered where would be best for our next charge, it dawned on me that it would take far too long to get to Portsmouth if we only used the free but slower chargers. There was, then, no option other than to pay for the rapid chargers, especially if we wanted to complete this part of the journey today, or this year, in fact.

Bingham, therefore, became our next stop at yet another supermarket, but this time it was Lidl. They had also spent a fair bit of money installing electric chargers at many of their stores, and I pondered that without these supermarkets, this journey might well be impossible even today, as the charging infrastructure is still more or less nonexistent in many areas. It seems to be constantly in the news about the need for a more effective charging network to encourage people to make the switch, but unfortunately, progress appears to be glacial at best.

As we left the city and drove around one of the many roundabouts for the seventh time just because I didn't know where I was going, we passed what looked like a huge First World War tank. Upon closer inspection, it turned out to be merely the façade of a tank, and it also turns out that Lincoln is actually the place where William Tritton and Walter Wilson holed up in a hotel room in 1915 for a few weeks while they came up with the design for the first-ever tank, which they decided to call Little Willie, presumably after consuming a bottle or two of something pretty strong. Unfortunately, Little Willie looks nothing like the depiction on the roundabout, but never mind, it does the job perfectly. Nevertheless, we were soon heading out of Lincoln via one or two diversions due to roadworks and were quickly heading towards Newark and then Bingham.

The main road we found ourselves on proved to be a faster road than what we had been used to, and the miles began to quickly disappear from the Leaf, though I was confident that we would not run out of juice. It wasn't as enjoyable a route, but we had spent half a day travelling just sixty miles, so it was good to put some distance between us and home. One interesting fact, though, is that this road, now known, quite boringly in my opinion, simply as the A46, is actually the Fosse Way, the longest road the Romans ever built on this little island of hours, and it went all the way from Lincoln to Exeter.

I tried to keep up with the traffic flow, as there is nothing worse than having a heavy goods vehicle right behind you, or worse, overtaking you, but this meant we used more fuel than if we had taken the minor roads. Soon enough, Newark flashed past us, and in what seemed like no time at all, we were pulling off the busy road and heading into Bingham itself, completely failing to see our destination. After a quick U-turn, we returned to the supermarket we had zoomed past and immediately found the charger in the far corner, thankfully shaded by some trees. The temperature had risen even further, so as Robin plugged the car in, we pulled a couple of camping chairs from the back seat and sat in the shade, trying to cool off. This was Robin's first lesson in charging electric cars. He took the cable out of the boot and tried to plug the wrong end into the car, which is impossible as it will simply not fit, but once he had figured out which end was which, he commented on how simple it was to do, as he had been expecting a much more complicated process. Once it was charging, though, we were in for a bit of a wait, as this charger was of the free but slow type, so I grabbed my map book and tried to figure out where the nearest rapid charger was.

I found a Nissan dealer in Loughborough, listed as having one rapid and five regular chargers, and decided to ring them. When I had first bought my Leaf, I had regularly dropped in for a quick charge when passing by my local Nissan showroom, and at first, they were more than willing to let the public do this. However, as the years have gone on, it has become increasingly difficult to charge at dealerships, either because the points are already occupied when you arrive or reserved for fleet vehicles. Some dealerships even state that chargers are no longer for public use, which is probably not surprising considering the ever-increasing number of electric vehicles on the road.

The call was answered immediately, and after a short conversation with a very helpful lady, she confirmed that, yes, we could call in and use their rapid charger. Quickly working out how many miles it was, around forty, I figured that we had around an hour to wait while the slow charger pumped enough juice into our battery to get us there and give us a couple of miles extra, just in case.

Rob and I took turns to wander into the supermarket, and although I bought a couple of drinks, the intention was just to enjoy the air-conditioning that the place offered. We sat in the shade of the trees and chatted for a while, and both agreed that we would have to figure out how to travel quicker, but to be honest, the hour soon passed, and we found ourselves back on the road again in what seemed like no time at all.

As we wandered slowly south on the A46, my satnav started to show some strange behaviour. I'm guessing that the roads around here must have been updated or re-routed at some point because, according to the map on the screen, we were happily driving through fields in excess of fifty miles per hour.

We gave up on using the in-car satnav, and Rob navigated us with his phone instead, and we were soon back on track. The countryside of Leicestershire was as beautiful as any we had seen so far, and when we turned off the main road to join the minor roads heading for Loughborough, we once again enjoyed stunning woods and hills complete with twists and turns galore.

I had never really been to Loughborough, so I had to rely completely on Rob to navigate us safely through the streets. All was going well until he told me to turn left, but when I did so, he said he had meant the other left and said I should have gone right instead. Apparently, he had stopped looking at the map on his phone, just for a minute, he had said, and had been watching a funny cat video. It's not necessarily Rob's fault, though. With enough computing power to get us to the moon, humans are just suckers when it comes to cats on film and instead just use their phones for watching such stuff. Even Thomas Edison, the prolific inventor responsible for finally bringing such things into our lives as light bulbs, movie cameras, and even car batteries, was guilty of this himself, recording his famous boxing cats way back in 1894. The animal rights people would go nuts nowadays, but it's worth a watch nonetheless. Regardless, I reminded Rob that we only had nine miles left on the car, and we didn't really want to drive any unnecessary miles, so I flung the car around in the road and gave Robin my best dirty look.

We arrived at the dealership with just six miles left and thankfully found the rapid charger to be free. I plugged in and followed the instructions on-screen, scanned my bank card to pay for the charge, heard a satisfying beep, then . . . nothing.

The car did not charge, no lights lit up, nothing. I tried again with the same outcome and wondered if there was a problem with my bank card, so I tried my credit card though with the same result.

A salesman came out to talk to us and said that the machine had been out of order for weeks. This was a bit of a blow, particularly as we had phoned in advance, as we had not only been hoping for a rapid charge to speed up our journey, but we were seriously low on charge. I tried ringing the operator of the charger. Still, after 15 minutes of being told how important my call was, which was obviously not very, I gave up. Instead, we managed to persuade the dealership to let us plug into their slow charger to give us enough juice to go somewhere else.

While the car slowly charged up, we took advantage of the dealer's air conditioning and facilities and figured there was another rapid charger just a couple of miles up the road. This wasn't a Pod Point charger, though, and we had to use a different app to find it. That app would be Zap-Map, which aims to locate as many chargers as possible on one map, regardless of which company they belong to.

Even though the car had only been plugged in for a few minutes, we were confident that we had enough electricity to get there, so we thanked them and left. At the back of my mind, I knew that

I could ring Green Flag if we ran out of fuel completely, but this was the last thing I wanted. Not only would it be dangerous to run out of fuel on a main road, or any road for that matter, by the time we would be picked up and towed to a charger, we could have covered many miles, and our progress was already painfully slow.

Rob navigated us through the still unfamiliar streets of Loughborough, which were now pretty busy as we were beginning to approach the start of the afternoon and evening rush hour, but after a few left and right turns, which Robin thankfully got right this time, we found ourselves at a Harvester pub, with a nice new rapid charger in the car park. I have to admit that I did take a right turn where I should not have really done so, and I apologise to the cyclist who commented on my mistake very verbally and would like to thank him for his kind and generous hand signals too.

I didn't get my hopes up at this charger, just in case, but plugged in anyway, scanned my bank card, and breathed a huge sigh of relief as the car finally started to charge. We had been down to four miles according to the car, which is cutting it about as close as I wished to get on this journey, it has to be said.

We ventured into the pub, and Rob got us a coke each, which was ridiculously expensive but offered free refills. It was nice to be in a cool building once again, as the heat remained as oppressive as ever outside, and as we sat staring out of the window and chatting, we noticed it had started to rain.

Unfortunately, I had left the windows open to keep the car cool, so I immediately jumped up and ran back to try to close them. Perhaps now would be a good point to mention the problems I have had with this car, which will not take long as there have only been two of them in four years.

During the dark days of the last winter, my car went crazy. I mean that in the most literal sense, as just before Christmas, I parked it up on my drive and locked it for the night. At around 11pm, we were drawn outside by an alien spaceship landing noisily in the garden. When we got out there, it turned out that the spaceship was my car. Flashing headlights and the beeping of a horn had certainly got our attention, which was very strange as the car was turned off and empty.

I unlocked it, sat behind the wheel, and tried to figure out how to turn everything off, which was difficult because, as I have already said, nothing was turned on. The windscreen wipers then joined in, at which point I figured the only thing to do would be to disconnect the battery, which obviously killed everything.

The next day, I reconnected the battery, and everything seemed well for a few days, but then the car began to behave strangely once again. I had my local mechanic look at it, but he just shuddered and said he didn't know much about electric cars and advised me to take it to the main dealer. I had been reluctant to do this, as I didn't fancy parting with my entire life savings, but when the strange behaviour continued and even worsened, I had no choice.

I remember the day I dropped it off at my local Nissan dealer very clearly. Once again, the headlights, horn and windscreen wipers all seemed to be having a party as I talked to the lady on the reception, or at least I tried to, as her attention was clearly on the little blue car going berserk somewhere in the background. Bizarrely, I had even disconnected the battery once again, which made no difference on this occasion, something which I still find very odd to this day, and I figured that the car was possessed by a demon or something similarly mischievous.

To cut a long story short, water had somehow managed to get through the seal of the windscreen and had collected on something called the Body Control Module, which is basically the brain of the car, and had clearly done some damage, so the car effectively had brain damage, poor thing. A new computer, windscreen, and a hefty bill later, I was pleased to say that the problem was solved, and although this little episode had cost a fair sum of money, I reminded myself that I had basically been enjoying free motoring for several years.

The second problem, though much less serious,

had only started a couple of weeks ago. I had opened the driver's electric window and turned the car off, as it had been a hot day, but when I turned the car back on, the window no longer seemed to work. This was a problem, I thought to myself, as the window was literally wide open, but as I repeatedly pressed the button to wind it up, I noticed it did move almost imperceptibly upwards, but only a fraction of a millimetre with each press. I must have pressed that button about a hundred times, but it was worth it, as I did eventually managed to close it completely. Not having had that problem fixed, it now became an issue in the rain today, as I sat there pressing it time and time again as the rain blew through it. By the time the window was closed, I was dripping wet, and my car seat was soaked, and ironically, as soon as I had managed to shut it, it stopped raining, which is just typical, I thought.

When I went back into the pub to finish my coke, I must have looked like a drowned rat. The lady greeting customers clearly did not remember me but just looked at me as if I was some kind of wild man who had dragged himself in from off the street, and for a moment, I thought she was going to stop me from coming back in completely. When I sat down, Rob just looked at me and laughed, and I thought that with friends like him, who needs enemies.

We finished our drinks and ventured back outside

to find the car almost fully charged. Because it was an incredibly hot day, the range shown by the car had gone up to 82 miles, though in reality, this would probably be around 50. However, this allowed us to make a big jump to the next charging point, where we would hopefully get another fast charge and would then be able to make up some quick miles. We had been driving for around six or seven hours but had only covered around 150 miles, and we still had around another hundred to go if we wished to get to the south coast today, which we most certainly wanted to do. As we drove out of the town, the rain once again started to fall, which quickly turned into hailstones, and the sound on the roof of the car was unbelievable. For a short while, the ground was white over, and at one point, I thought the hailstones were going to smash through the car's windscreen.

We headed south again, with noticeably more traffic on the roads, and got stuck in some rush-hour antics as we trundled through Coventry. Coventry is not a place I am familiar with, but I can tell you one thing, it has a higher concentration of roundabouts than any other location in the universe, I imagine. It was literally roundabout after roundabout, and I particularly enjoyed the guessing game of which lane to choose at each one, which was less a game of skill and more of a lottery, I can tell you. Whoever planned the city's urban sprawl and its roads perhaps had shares in tarmac or concrete, or was maybe going for a new Guinness world record for the number of round-abouts on a five-mile stretch of road. This is why I mentioned earlier that I thought it quite fitting that our route would take us on an almost perfect circle around the city, which is perhaps art imitating life, or is it the other way around?

Anyway, I should perhaps, at this instant, take the opportunity to apologise to the elderly lady in the red Vauxhall who I may or may not have cut up slightly or a lot when leaving the city. On the other hand, I would also like to say that she has a rather interesting and intriguing collection of hand signals, and I suspect she used all of them towards me, and I am still trying to figure out which hand signal goes with which swear word. Regardless, I deserved it.

I lost count of the number of roundabouts at 30, which was when granny was gesticulating towards me and was when Robin had his eyes shut in fear, but these are the risks of driving on roads that you are unfamiliar with, I'm afraid. It's also a good thing that Rob was bald because any hair would have fallen out anyway with my driving that day.

Somehow or other, we survived Coventry, and early in the evening, we trundled into the car park of Tesco at Southam, just east of Royal Leamington Spa. I wondered if we were now technically in the south of England, and I suspected that the answer was yes, though opinion differs drastically on this subject. I know someone who lives in Leicester, and he considers himself a northerner, and I could spend many hours trying to figure out where the south stops and the north starts, but there you go.

Southam had the luxury of one rapid charger and four regular chargers, but only the rapid was available, which was lucky for us. I plugged in, waited for the beep, and scanned my card, but nothing happened, so I tried again. This time, the charge started, but stopped after just a few seconds, so once again, I unplugged and reset the charger to give it another go. This continued for quite a while. Only two attempts had successfully started after attempting to charge six or seven times, but both stopped after a few seconds.

A young man was charging his Tesla in one of the regular chargers next to us, and as he wound his window down, which worked perfectly by the way and was in no way broken, he told us that the last person who had tried to charge there had also seemed to have problems. He said he was leaving now anyway, so we could have his spot, but of course, this meant that we would have a longer wait than expected to gain a sufficient charge. We thanked him anyway, moved the car into the next spot, plugged in and went into Tesco to enjoy their air conditioning. While we were in there, I accidentally bought a bottle of wine, and Rob bought a watermelon, of all things.

We once again got our camping chairs out of the

car and made ourselves comfortable in the car park, enjoying the warm evening sunshine. Rob produced a large machete, which would probably have alarmed any shoppers had they have seen it, and he then proceeded to slice the watermelon up in military fashion.

I do notice that whenever we go camping, Rob seems to have every tool imaginable that you could possibly need, which is good because I am something of a useless camper, it has to be said. Still, I was very surprised by the machete, but it certainly did the job. While we were sat there, we might have been given a few strange looks by passers-by who were simply there to do their shopping, but we did not care, and anyway, we were used to being stared at.

Luckily, the next available fast charger was just a short hop away at Banbury in Oxfordshire, approximately fifteen miles away. After an hour of relaxing in the car park and eating watermelon, we reckoned there was enough charge in the old Leaf to get us there, and we would even have a few spare miles just in case of any diversions or other problems along the way. It is fair to say that electric cars charge quicker when the batteries are nearly empty, and the charging rate slows down as they reach their full capacity, which is why we only had to wait an hour or so to make sure we had enough juice.

As we left Southam heading, well, south, I was

surprised to see a sign for Bishop's Itchington and figured it was a real place after all, and the train lady had not lied to me, although it wasn't going to form any other part of our journey today. The road was pretty light of traffic, and in no time at all, we were pulling into yet another Tesco, this time on the outskirts of Banbury. There was no doubt that we were definitely in the south of England now, and the weather confirmed this. It was now early evening, yet the sun was as strong as ever, and as I plugged the car in and prayed for the rapid charger to work, I could feel the sun's rays warming my skin.

All the bleeps and sounds suggested that the rapid charger was indeed working, and as the lights on the leaf itself lit up, telling us that the car definitely was charging, we headed into the store to use the facilities and to cool off by climbing in with the ice-cream. We both came out with yet more stuff, Robin with crisps and me with a couple of drinks, and I wondered how much we were spending by continually going into supermarkets and buying assorted junk food, drinks and everything else, and whether or not it would have been cheaper to just pay for petrol. I guess by having these chargers, though, customers will be encouraged to shop here if they have electric cars rather than shop at a store without them. It's just a no brainer. I mean, why wouldn't you take advantage of free fuel for your car?

The rapid charger soon had the leaf more or less full again, and after consulting our map, we decided to head for Wallingford, just north of Reading, which promised a rapid charge at a Lidl supermarket. Slowly, almost imperceptibly, it was beginning to get dark as we drove into the town, and as the car charged, our thoughts turned to where we were going to sleep for the night. We had brought tents and sleeping bags but had not come across any campsites yet, so we decided to look for a suitable spot as soon as the car was charged.

Unfortunately, it seemed to get really dark really quickly, and as we left town, it was almost impossible to see anything at all beyond the headlight beams of the car. A quick search for a campsite nearby brought up nothing, so we decided to continue south, confident that we would just come across a suitable spot.

Unfortunately, this was not to be, so around 10.30pm, we pulled off the main road onto a pitch-black country lane, wondering whether or not we would be sleeping in the car that night. Luckily, after just a few hundred yards, an even smaller, darker lane promised an empty farmer's field, and as I pulled the car in, we decided that this was our only choice. We parked the car and got out to survey the area around it, and there did appear to be just enough room to put our tents up, though the grass was a little too long. We were fully committed, however, so, in short order, we soon had the tents up, our chairs out, and we were sat enjoying a nice bottle of beer under the stars almost exactly in the middle of nowhere.

The tents had been a bit of a struggle to put up. We had each brought our own two-man tent, chiefly so I didn't have to put up with Rob's snoring among the many other sounds he makes in the night, and both were brand new and identical. Although I had briefly put my tent up once before, Rob had never had his out of the bag, and anyway, I had forgotten how to put it up. Fumbling around in the dark, though, we somehow managed it, though mine looked a decidedly poor effort compared to Rob's.

All around us could be heard the sounds of animals and birds, with the sound of the traffic in the distance more or less a quiet whisper, and a couple of satellites passed overhead as we chatted about our day. Although we had not made it to the south coast, we figured we were not far off, so at some point just after 11pm, we turned in for the night, absolutely shattered. We unanimously decided that travelling like this was truly exhausting.

Unfortunately, it seems that 11pm is the time when the countryside comes alive at night. As soon as we had zipped up safely in our tents, I could hear owls in the trees and some kind of large creature, probably a bear, schnaffling around outside. Of course, I didn't get out, not that I was scared, but I was just too exhausted to move, honest.

The road sounds became noisier, too, with lorries apparently pushing their engines to the limit to get up nearby hills, and every now and then, it was possible to hear cars passing over a level crossing that we had gone by earlier. I also wondered whether or not a tractor would squash us in the night, as we were in a farmer's field after all, but figured that we would not know anything about it and went to sleep.

THE TURNAROUND

The good thing about camping is that you are up nice and early, but the bad thing about camping is that you are up nice and early. I first looked at my watch at around 4.30am, a time in the morning that I do not recall ever having encountered before. I did not move out of principle, as it was just such a silly time to get up, but it was already bright daylight, so I was forced to move after just fifteen minutes.

It's probably a good job I did. When I popped my head out of the tent, our middle of nowhere was nothing of the sort, and there was a farmhouse just thirty yards away. I don't think we actually camped in the farmer's garden, but we might as well have, so I suggested to Rob that we pack up and disappear before he came to shoot us.

Everything was a bit wet, so I didn't pack my tent properly but just shoved it into the footwell of the back seat, intending to dry it later. Rob did the same, and within just a few minutes, we were once again in the car and heading south, this time towards Hook, just east of Basingstoke and at the other side of Reading.

Reading was not a place that was familiar to me, I thought to myself as we drove through it at around 5am, but it did seem to have a lot of big roads, though its roundabouts were far inferior to those found in Coventry. We almost took a wrong turn when Rob got his left and right mixed up once again, but somehow managed to stay on track, and by around 5.30am, we were parked up in a Tesco, with the car plugged in, our tents hanging out to dry and, get this, Robin had not one but two stoves on the go and was simultaneously cooking us a sausage sandwich and making us a cup of coffee. Did I mention that I plugged the car in, though? I like to do my bit.

Once again, early morning shoppers were giving us strange looks, but I reckoned it should have been us looking at them in a suspicious manner because what kind of person goes shopping at this time of the day? A couple of the more friendly types stopped to talk to us, and they were very polite, but one of them was looking at my sausage sandwich in a manner that was quite frankly very rude. As we sat eating, I tried to find out a bit about Hook, but there wasn't much to say about it, other than the place had murdered Thomas Burberry, founder of the clothing empire that still bears his name, and who had died here in 1926.

The map suggested we were now within easy reach of the south coast, so once we had tidied up all our mess and packed our now-dry tents away, we hit the road again. Farnham was the next stop, at yet another Lidl, but this was a rapid charger, so it was only a ten-minute stop, and when we got going again, we had Portsmouth in our sights.

We were on the A3, which took us directly towards the city, but being a faster road, we watched the battery level drop remarkably quickly. However, because we had kept the battery topped up, there was no real concern over getting to where we were going or having any problem charging when we got there as there were plenty of charging points in the town.

Our first sight of the sea was very satisfying, and Rob and I saw it simultaneously, with us acting in a manner that was probably a bit like how children behave on a school trip. The traffic going into the city was relatively light, and it was quite a pleasant drive as well. Rob guided us to the car park, yet another Tesco, and though this was another slow charger, it was not a problem as we planned to walk into the city centre to have a look around anyway.

I had been to Portsmouth a couple of times previously and had very much enjoyed the historic naval dockyard that houses HMS Victory, which was exactly where we were heading now. Rob had never seen it and wanted to have a look, so after we parked up, we were straight off on our short walk to the waterfront.

Portsmouth certainly appears to have some money, as when we finally found ourselves in the city centre, we stumbled across Gunwharf Quays, a high-end shopping centre if ever there was one. We figured the money came mainly from the naval base, and I imagined it was probably quite a nice place to live. There was lots of al-fresco dining, and most of the streets were pedestrian-friendly, but we were there for one reason only, so Rob could see HMS Victory.

As well as being the Royal Navy's most famous warship, HMS Victory is also a beautiful work of art, in my mind at least, but the ship is also Lord Nelson's famous flagship from the Battle of Trafalgar. Admiral Horatio Nelson had been in command of his fleet from the deck of Victory, but on 21 October 1805, towards the end of the battle, he was shot while on the deck of his ship by a sneaky French sniper. He survived for a few hours, long enough to hear that the battle had been victorious, but died later that afternoon. To say that his death overshadowed the victory of the battle would be an understatement, and when news of his demise reached the country, the whole nation went into mourning. He was only 47 years old as well.

Unfortunately for Rob, however, the cunning people that run the historic dockyard have made sure that the only way to see the ship is to pay the hefty entrance fee, so we walked all the way there and back for nothing, though we did see HMS

Warrior instead, a very nice ship in itself, but just not quite as good as the Victory. Rob will have to make a return visit one day and dip into his pocket somewhat.

As we walked back to the car, Rob and I discussed the fact that the most interesting part of this journey was about to begin. Over the last few months, we meticulously researched some of the more interesting and unusual places to visit, which just happened to be on or incredibly close to the watershed route that separates the rivers flowing east from the rivers flowing west. This underlines something that I have said on many occasions before, which is that we are lucky to live on our historic little island as we do. It is my firm belief that you could literally draw any line on a map anywhere in this country and follow it. You will undoubtedly come across many fine places with countless amazing stories to tell if you do so, and this trip is going to be no different.

We chose to start here for no reason other than it is sort of on the centre of the south coast, and would be a sensible place to start a journey that goes right up the centre of England. The first step is to actually get to the coast itself, though, so with a fully charged car, we head to the tiny village of Warsash, just to the west of Portsmouth and overlooking the beautiful River Hamble. There is a car park on the waterfront just next to the Rising Sun pub, and as we get out of the car, the heat was once again intolerable, though there was a nice breeze coming from the water. You could choose to start from many other places that are all also on some kind of watershed line, but this one just made sense to us.

To be honest, there is not a lot here, but the views are nice over the river, especially towards the village of Hamble-le-Rice. Although we were not going across the river, because that is entirely the point of this journey, Hamble-le-Rice is an interesting place in itself and is where a guy called Sir Edwin Alliott Verdon-Roe is buried over at St Andrew's Church. If you have never heard of him, this is the man that, as well as having a fancy name, in 1908 designed, built and flew his own plane, becoming the first Englishman to do so. He went on to form the Avro Company, which basically suggests his initials, and by 1914 he was selling his Avro 504 to anyone who wanted one. This was your classic biplane, and quite frankly, was soon outdated, but it did gain two major distinctions. It was both the first-ever British plane to be shot down, which he probably didn't shout about, but it was also the plane that was used in the first-ever air-raid, bombing the Zeppelin works on the shores of Lake Constance in the deep south of Germany, which is quite a feat you have to admit. If that's not interesting to you, then you might find it amusing that Hamble-le-Rice is also the place that notorious London gangsters Ronnie and Reggie Kray would come to every year for their summer holiday, which kind of makes you wonder who or what is buried under all that sand.

Just to the southeast, if you look really carefully, a small buoy marks the spot where the Mary Rose sank. The Mary Rose was, of course, the flagship of the English fleet and the favourite of the king himself, none other than Henry VIII, and she sank out there in July 1545. It is said that she sank because her gun ports had been left open, which is a bit embarrassing quite frankly, and although there is a common misconception that she sank on her initial voyage, she actually served the king well for around 34 years, being launched from Portsmouth around 1511.

Anyway, all of that aside, it is time to move on, so we hop back into the car and, for the first time, find ourselves heading north towards a place called Hambledon. The idea is to work our way up the Meon Valley, or just to the west of it, as the watershed lies in that area. However, we will allow ourselves to deviate a couple of miles on either side to take in interesting places along the way, and as we head towards Hambledon, we come across our first such stop.

Fort Nelson is an impressive fort and is one of five that the Victorians placed along the top of Portsdown Hill to counter any French invasion threat. The Prime Minister, Lord Palmerston, had long warned of the risk of French invasion and insisted that their hate of the English meant that they would love to *inflict a deep humiliation* on us. Furthermore, the French launched the world's first ironclad, *Le Gloire*, or *Glory*, in 1859, worrying everybody, including Queen Victoria herself, although this ship was quickly rendered obsolete by HMS Warrior's launch in 1860, which was the world's first armour-plated iron-hulled warship and which we saw earlier in Portsmouth if you remember. Nonetheless, the forts were built anyway, along with many along the south coast, and although they later came to be known as *Palmerston's Folly*, it is perhaps their very presence that persuaded the French not to invade or attack at the time.

The fort remains as impressive nowadays as it was when it was built, and I had the pleasure of getting a look behind the scenes there a couple of years ago when I worked for the Royal Armouries. As well as the national artillery collection being stored there, the fort also houses one other, less well-known curiosity: a small jar of metal fragments. It might not look much, but that little jar of metal fragments is the first example of shrapnel, collected from the exploding shell designed and built by Henry Shrapnel, where it obviously got its name.

We had a look around the fort, which was free to get into, and also managed to get a good look at the gun carriage that carried Queen Victoria's body at her funeral, and saw a piece of the Iraqi supergun that became so famous in the scandal of the 1990s, but we then decided that we must move on, although we could have spent all day in there.

There are good views of Portsmouth from the top of Portsdown Hill, so before we left, we made sure to have a good look, and I imagined that it would also be a very fine view at night. I closed my eyes to try to recreate the effect, but it just wasn't the same.

Before we leave Portsmouth behind forever, there are a few things worth mentioning, which are quite interesting. For instance, Portsmouth FC is the record holder for hanging onto the FA Cup for the longest time, which is nothing to do with them being really good at football but is because the Second World War broke out while it was in their possession after they beat Wolverhampton Wanderers in 1939. During the war, and to keep the cup safe, it somehow ended up in the Bird in Hand pub, where it was kept under the landlord's bed every night. Portsmouth also gave us the umbrella, without which us Brits would be in a spot of bother no doubt. I say it gave us the umbrella, but Jonas Hanway from the city was reported to be the first person to use a parasol to protect himself from the rain. He got the idea when he saw women in the far east using parasols to protect themselves from the sun, and you can only wonder why nobody managed to figure this out any earlier, really. Lastly, that fine city below us is where Sir Arthur Conan Doyle wrote his first Sherlock Holmes story – A

Study in Scarlet, published in 1887. Apparently, he based Dr Watson on his friend, a real doctor who was the president of Portsmouth's Literary Society, so there you go.

Hambledon proved to be only a short drive away, and when we got there, we still had plenty of miles left on the battery. Parking at the top of a shallow hill near the church, I wanted to come here to see if there was any trace of a man called William Lashley, who was born, lived and died here. While that might not make him sound all that remarkable, he certainly was, as at some point, he found the time to leave this beautiful little corner of Hampshire to go exploring with none other than Captain Robert Falcon Scott on a couple of polar expeditions.

The first one, the Discovery Expedition, was unremarkable, but on the second one, the Terra Nova Expedition, he nearly died along with all of his comrades. The primary aim of the expedition had been to discover the South Pole before anyone else, so I imagine that Captain Scott was somewhat annoyed when he finally made it to the pole, where the only thing he discovered was a Norwegian flag sticking out of the ice and fluttering in the wind and a few empty tins of kippers.

Regardless of that, however, Lashley soon found himself in his own sticky situation. He was a member of the last support team to be sent back by Scott on his quest for the pole, along with Edward Evans and Tom Crean. Evans became struck down by scurvy on the journey back, but Lashley and Crean refused to leave him behind, dragging him for a further 65 miles. At this point, the party only had two days of rations left but still had four- or five-days sledge pulling to contend with, so Lashley stayed with Evans while Crean set out alone to raise the alarm. He somehow managed to walk the last 35 miles in 18 hours, after which a rescue party was sent to save Lashley and Evans. Lashley wrote about his experiences, and his account was published in a book amusingly called *The Worst Journey in the World*.

Lashley, not surprisingly, never went anywhere near the Antarctic ever again, and can you really blame him, and he retired to his house back in the village of his birth. The house was called Minna Bluff and is quite distinctive, sporting two tall chimneys and sitting on the north side of West Street. I was tempted to knock on the door, but for some reason, I decided not to, probably because I am conscious of the fact that I slept in a field last night and have not had a proper wash.

It is only a short drive from here to Droxford, which is another example of a tiny English village having links with the history of the world. We parked just near the phone box and strolled to the bench that will begin to tell this little story. On the bench, there is a plaque. It states that none other than Winston Churchill made his headquarters at Droxford in the days leading up to 6th June

1944, which was, of course, D-Day and the allied invasion of Europe. Churchill rolled into Droxford on his armoured train, and this village had been chosen as it offered a good place to hide a train in the wooded valleys that dominate this area. General Eisenhower and Charles De Gaulle also attended, along with many other wartime leaders, and there is a funny story that tells how angry De Gaulle became when Churchill told him that France would be invaded within the next few days, as up until this point, no one had bothered to tell him. He never forgave us for this, and that is partly why, as president of the French Republic, he twice vetoed Britain's entry into the EEC in 1963 and 1967. He distrusted us and thought we would always take the American side of any argument, and we only managed to join after France elected a new president in 1969 and De Gaulle died in 1970.

We had a walk to find the old train station, which is now a private house, but on the letterbox outside, another plaque told us that Churchill spent some time here. There is a story that this is where he decided to postpone the invasion due to bad weather, but it is more likely that that decision was taken at Southwick House, some 9 miles south of here and back towards Portsmouth. Still, Droxford is a very nice village, and many important decisions would certainly have been taken here at the time, immortalising Droxford in history forever, I guess.

The drive out of Droxford was very pleasant, taking us through yet more small woods and along lanes bordered by high hedges, though occasional glimpses of the wider countryside showed it to be beautiful. We were stuck behind a tractor after Corhampton, but this just allowed us to enjoy the view as the high hedges had disappeared, and when it finally turned off, we found we were at our next destination, which was West Meon just a few miles up the road.

Travelling today was much less stressful than yesterday when we had constantly wondered where we would next charge, and both Rob and I had relaxed considerably this morning. We parked on Church Lane, as it was the church where we were heading to and admired the beautiful thatched cottages that seemed to form the centre of the village. We walked up to the pub, the Thomas Lord, which gives away one of the village's secrets, as this is where the founder of Lord's Cricket Ground retired in 1830, and he could not have picked a finer spot. We had a swift half-pint of coke inside, more to make use of the facilities than anything else, and then had a wander down to the church, St John's, on the outskirts of the village and back near where we had parked.

Here, the second secret of West Meon is to be found in the form of a cross bearing the name Guy Burgess. Burgess was a cold war spy and was one of the most successful the Russians ever managed to recruit. He came from good stock, with his father being a high-ranking naval officer and his mother an aristocrat, so he was accepted into the upper echelons of British society almost without question.

Recruited while at university, he joined the BBC and then worked for various politicians, and at the outset of the Second World War, he joined British Intelligence. After the war, he became a diplomat and managed to pass all sorts of secrets to the Russians before the whole affair unravelled in 1951 when he became a suspect, along with his friends Kim Philby and Donald Maclean, who had both also enjoyed successful careers and rapid promotions because of their social backgrounds.

Burgess escaped to Russia, drank himself first into a depression and then to death, after which his body was returned to England for burial right here, in the family plot. Looking around at the peaceful and serene churchyard today, you would never associate it with such intrigue, but there you go.

We were just a few miles west of Petersfield, which was to be our next destination, and when we got back in the car, we decided that we had plenty of miles left, so we looked to see where else we could go on the way. We also wanted to visit Winchester, which was off to the west, so we decided to go there instead and return to Petersfield later. Unfortunately, these two towns were in opposite directions, so there was no other way of doing it, but we figured we could get a charge in both of them anyway.

We headed to Martins Nissan on the outskirts of this small city, and the staff were very helpful and let us plug in without any hesitation. A short walk took us past a Tesla dealer, where I eyed up my next car, and we were soon in the city centre, which was particularly full today as it looked like there was a graduation ceremony taking place. Many well-dressed parents wandered alongside students clad in traditional caps and gowns, and after a quick look around the city centre, which was both compact and beautiful, we headed for the cathedral. As we sat in the shade of some trees, Rob was asked by a young lady to take a photo of her and her family, while, as usual, I sat and did nothing.

As Rob did his best impression of being a photographer, and after I shouted at him to make sure to get their feet in, I remembered what I had read about Winchester and how it was once the ancient capital of England. It is rich in history, and if you do want to pop inside the castle just around the corner, as we did, you can see King Arthur's Round Table, but don't get too excited as it is a mere replica of the original, apparently. Even so, it is around 700 years old and has reportedly been hanging on the wall there since 1348. From a distance, it looks like a huge dartboard, and who knows, maybe it was?

The cathedral is interesting, too. As I sat looking at it today, there is no indication that it was quite literally sinking into the ground until relatively recently. Royal Navy diver William Walker volunteered to spend 6 years shoring up the foundations with concrete and bricks. He was not by himself, of course. That would be just silly. His 150-man team, and it was all men, I'm afraid to say, spent 6 years and used 25,000 bags of concrete, 150,000 concrete blocks, 900,000 bricks, and a similar amount of beer presumably, fixing the foundations. They certainly did a good job.

There are countless famous people buried here, too. King Cnut is famous for failing to turn back the sea and is in there somewhere, though his story is often mistold. He is said to have failed to turn back the tide, but modern historians claim that he was demonstrating to those around him that even a King had limits to his powers, chiefly because he was sick of all of those around him telling him how wonderful he was all the time.

The original version of the story, however, has Cnut placing his chair on the shore, possibly near Southampton, and commanding the tide to halt, but after it obviously failed to do so, he declared that all the world should know that the power of kings is empty and worthless, and he never wore his crown again.

Interestingly, old Cnut's bones are now a bit mixed up with those of a guy called William Rufus, who, as well as having a cool name, was also the third son of William the Conqueror. This mix-up occurred because during the English Civil War, plundering Roundheads, who were on the side of the Parliamentarians and hence hated the King and everything he stood for, raided the cathedral and scattered Cnut's bones all over the place just because he was a king. It was not until the restoration of the monarchy some years later that someone sorted them out again, but no one really knows how good a job they did.

Another great king, Alfred the Great, in fact, was also buried here. I say *was* because at some point, they sort of lost him. I'm not sure how easy it is to lose a body, particularly one belonging to a king, but nonetheless, they did a sterling job of it back then, and nobody knows where he ultimately ended up. Perhaps he will turn up underneath a car park one day, as Richard III did recently in Leicester, which was incidentally probably quite a surprise for the parking attendant, but for the foreseeable future at least, Alfred's whereabouts remain a mystery.

Lastly, a couple of others are worth a quick mention, though neither are royalty. If you are a fan of Jane Austen, though, she is somewhere underneath my feet, and as far as I know, her remains have neither been lost nor desecrated. However, perhaps not the most famous but certainly the most interesting grave here is that of a man called

Thomas Thetcher, also known as the Hampshire Grenadier. Don't worry, I had never heard of him either, but his story is fascinating, I promise. If you do happen to find yourself here, then make time to go and have a look at his grave, which reads like an eye test with the writing getting smaller as it goes down the stone.

His grave went on to inspire many people after it was noticed by a man called Bill Wilson, an American, who had the misfortune to find himself over here on his way to fight in the trenches of the First World War. The story goes that Bill was wandering around the graveyard prior to his deployment when he stumbled across the grave. When he found himself having problems with alcohol a few years later, he remembered it, and it had left such an impression on him that he went on to found Alcoholics Anonymous. To this day, the wording from Thomas Thetcher's gravestone features on page one of the AA's Big Book, albeit in a slightly misquoted form:

> *Here lies a Hampshire Grenadier*
>
> *Who caught his death*
>
> *Drinking cold small beer*
>
> *A good soldier is ne'er forgot*
>
> *Whether he dieth by musket*
>
> *Or by pot'*

Regardless of accuracy, Thomas Thetcher was

clearly well-loved by his comrades, who paid for his gravestone, and the one you see today, if you come here that is, is actually the fifth stone to stand on this spot, having been erected in 1966.

We had spent enough time in Winchester, though, so after a quick walk back up the steep hill to Martins Nissan, and after thanking them for the free charge, we hopped into the car and headed straight to Petersfield, which was just twenty miles away.

We passed West Meon once again, or at least close by it, and half an hour later, we were parking up in the car park of yet another Tesco, this one in the heart of the town. I was dismayed to find that you had to pay to park here, which was a first on this trip, but on a positive note, this meant that there was no time limit, so we would have plenty of time to do what we wanted to do here, which was just one thing.

I grew up watching films such as the Ealing comedies, with my favourite being *The Lavender Hill Mob*, and went on to watch such greats as *The Bridge on the River Kwai*, which I had actually always thought was called *The Bridge Over the River Kwai*, how wrong was I, and of course, probably my favourite, *Lawrence of Arabia*. I probably don't need to mention that I also grew up with *Star Wars*, and if you haven't already figured it out, what these films all have in common is Sir Alec Guinness, who is possibly best remembered now for his role as Obi-Wan Kenobi. Well, it turns out that he is buried right here, in Petersfield cemetery, so on this hot summer's day, Rob and myself find ourselves on a pilgrimage to his grave.

Guinness was not just an actor, however. In 1943, for instance, he found himself on the frontline of the Second World War and in command of a landing craft during Operation Husky, which was the allied invasion of Sicily. Later on in the war, he spent his time smuggling secret agents into Yugoslavia, as it was then known, so he was altogether one heck of an interesting guy.

We should not take it for granted that Guinness chose to appear in the Star Wars movies either. In fact, we should be grateful that he did because things could have been very different. The actor wasn't very keen when he initially read the script and even described it as *fairy tale rubbish*, but after the movie studio doubled his offer, he decided that it wasn't as rubbish as he had thought after all. This role made him not only famous to a new generation but also made him incredibly wealthy, though he was never what you would call happy about being identified with his character from the movie, which is unfortunate because that is exactly what happened for the rest of his life. He is even said to have been the one that suggested to George Lucas that Kenobi's character be killed off, as he was sick of his *bloody awful lines* and having to speak *mumbo jumbo*, his words not mine. He was, however, incredibly grateful for the financial security the role provided him and his family for the rest of his life, which allowed him to live in a relatively modest way, something that is clearly reflected in his gravestone, which can certainly be described as modest, and something which Robin and I both commented on.

I said there was only one thing we wanted to do while in Petersfield, but there is actually something else too, which I had almost forgotten about. Somewhere in this town, there is a bookshop, one of those old types that sell all sorts where you can have a proper rummage, but this one is different in that it is run by possibly the most recognisable football fan in the country. His name, and I kid you not about this, is *John Anthony Portsmouth Football Club Westwood*, which I presume must have involved a trip to see a solicitor at some point as I cannot imagine any mother allowing her child to be called that, no matter how big a football fan dad happened to be. We found the shop on Chapel Street, and it was exactly as described. Although the gentleman behind the counter was busy with another customer while we had a mooch around, it was clearly John, judging by the couple of tattoos that could just be seen depicting his beloved club.

A short walk back to the car saw us wandering through some nice little back streets, and we stopped for a rest when we found a smart little garden on the High Street called Petersfield Physic Garden. This was a little oasis of shade, butterflies and robins, and was a welcome surprise where we could stop and rest and cool down a little while we considered our next steps. We still had many hours of daylight left and a fully charged car, hopefully, so although we certainly wanted to get a bit further before the day's end, we didn't want to end up in a field like we did last night, so we decided to come up with a better plan. The good thing about technology is that no matter where you are, it is now possible to search for a campsite at any time, and this is exactly what we did. We found one at the Crown Inn near Devizes and set ourselves the goal of getting there before the day was out, which would be a push, but we were sure we could do it.

With the car fully charged, we set off to our next stop, which should only be a brief one, to see an interesting church at West Tisted, which was probably less than ten miles away. Once again, the quiet roads proved to be fantastic, although they should be as we were now aware that we had been driving through the South Downs National Park for the last few miles. A nice wooded valley turned into open fields after a couple of miles, which was a welcome relief as the road had been pretty narrow and the visibility was bad, what with us humans not being able to see around bends.

We parked close to the church and spent a pleasant five minutes mooching around the churchyard, though the church itself was unfortunately locked. The interesting thing about this church, though, was its path, which crosses a moat, not something you see every day. Something else that you don't see every day is a 1,000-year-old yew tree, which was quite frankly rather more impressive than the moat bridge and resembled something out of Game of Thrones.

With everything to be seen taken care of, we hopped back into the car for a short ride to Ropley. The next few stops were all going to be brief, and Ropley would be no exception, as we just wanted to see a bridge. It was not any old bridge though, although it was indeed old, but this bridge was a film star and had been in Harry Potter.

We pulled up in the car park at Ropley Station, and as we jumped out, we saw a footbridge, but as Alec Guinness would say, this was not the bridge we were looking for. The one we wanted was a short walk to the east, and after just a couple of minutes, we were up the steps and at the top of it, waiting for any passing trains to come along.

This railway is a heritage line called the Watercress Line, presumably because the stuff was previously farmed around here. The bridge dates from 1893, when it was erected in King's Cross Station, where it later starred in the Harry Potter films, albeit in an uncredited role, obviously. The station took it down in 2009 as part of a modernisation programme, and it took nine lorries to transport it here, where it was restored, repainted and finally placed in the position which it still occupies today.

At the time, a station spokesperson said that the only people that used the bridge anymore were Harry Potter fans and staff, which basically means everyone when you think about it. While it is a shame it had to be removed then, it is at least a good thing that it found a new home here.

Almost giving up on seeing a train pass beneath the bridge and wanting to move on, and just as we were about to leave, we heard a whistle from behind us and decided to wait. Within a few minutes, a train was indeed approaching us, and while I am sad to say it was not the Hogwarts Express, I am delighted to report that it was none other than Thomas the Tank Engine. Priceless.

Jumping back in the car, we next headed to Four Marks, where we wanted to visit another part of the Watercress Line. This time we got lost, though, and ended up on a housing estate, although by some miracle, we eventually found ourselves to be right next to the station, which was called Medstead and Four Marks. Jumping out of the car and abandoning it in front of a tall hedge, we hopped over the railway line using yet another footbridge, this one pinched from Cowes on the Isle of Wight, and were soon stood on the station platform, patiently awaiting Thomas to catch us up. The reason we had wanted to visit this particular station was that it was so high. Not in the sense of any kind of drugs, silly, but in terms of height. At 650 feet above sea level, making it the highest station in southern England, it certainly sounded high, but as we stood on the platform today, there was no sense of height whatsoever. Also, while 650 feet might sound high, it is nothing on Dent station in Cumbria, which is a whopping 1,150 feet high, but even Dent station is beaten by Corrour on the West Highland Line, at a truly amazing 1,340 feet and the highest in the UK. Incidentally, Corrour is the train station used in the film Trainspotting, making it high in all senses of the word.

We were brought back into the now with a short toot-toot from Thomas' whistle, after which the little train puffed into the station and slowed to a halt. We waited while passengers variously jumped on or off, and when the train had shuffled off, we did exactly the same.

Back at the car, we were surprised to find a note stuck to our windscreen, and for a moment, I wondered if we had a secret admirer. Unfortunately, this was not the case, and although I am paraphrasing somewhat here, whoever left the note seemed to be inquiring whether or not it was Stevie Wonder who taught me to park. I looked at my feeble attempt and realised that, yes, I had indeed parked very crappily, although as there were literally no other cars around, I concluded that whoever left me this note was a bit of a jobsworth.

Leaving Four Marks and its nosey neighbour behind, it was but a short hop, skip and a jump into the small town of Alton. We had intended to grab a quick top-up charge here, albeit with a slow charger, as free electricity is free electricity, I had thought. However, when we arrived at the charger, which was situated in the car park of the local leisure centre, we discovered that it was not a free charger, after all, so we decided to wait as there was still plenty of miles left on the car, although obviously how many exactly was anybody's guess.

While here, however, we still decided to visit the grave of Fanny Adams, who hailed from this town. While you may not have heard of her as such, you have probably heard her name and are sat there right now wondering where you have heard it. Well, this is a very interesting story, although something of a sad one, so here we go, and please bear with me.

Fanny Adams was born here in 1859 and lived with her large family on Tanhouse Lane. She lived a happy and carefree life in what was up until then, a crime-free little town, and she was well-known in the area. However, her happy childhood ended one sunny afternoon in August 1867, after she had gone out playing in a place called Flood Meadows, just at the end of her street and bordering the River Wey.

Fanny had been with her sister and a friend when a young man named Frederick Baker offered to buy the girls some sweets. Baker had been drinking, and when Fanny took his money but refused to go with him, he took her anyway, and she was never seen again, at least not alive and not in one piece. Fanny's friends ran home and told their story, which was originally dismissed out of hand, but as the evening drew in and Fanny still failed to come home, a search was organised, and attention began to focus on Baker and is where the story gets a bit dark.

To cut a long story short, Fanny's severed head was found on a hop pole, and her various limbs were later found scattered around the local area. Her internal organs had been removed, and some had been further desecrated, which all goes on to explain why this murder became one of the most notorious of the nineteenth century, along with the fact that several body parts were never found at all, which is an important point to remember for later on in this intriguing little tale.

Anyhow, hundreds of people had been involved in the search, which destroyed any possible evidence around the crime scene, but without their involvement, it is unlikely that so many body parts would have been recovered. Quite bizarrely, the parts that were recovered were then taken to a nearby house and sewn together, which must have been not only a gruesome and horrendous sight but also a gruesome and horrendous job.

With Baker as the only suspect, he was quickly arrested, probably for his own good, as a large mob had gathered outside the solicitor's office where he worked. When he was searched, Baker had blood on his clothes, and he was in possession of two knives. However, when police searched his workplace, it was his diary that gave him away. The entry for Saturday 24th August 1867 read simply *Killed a young girl. It was fine and hot.* Eyewitnesses later pinned him to the location on the day of the murder, and although forensic science at the time was in its infancy, traces of blood found on Baker's knives and clothes was determined to be human.

At his trial, his defence counsel argued that his diary entry was somehow not a confession, which was always going to be a stretch, I imagine, but the jury disagreed and took only fifteen minutes to find him guilty. He was hanged in Winchester on Christmas Eve, and the notoriety of the crime attracted a crowd of 5,000. With his hanging being the last public execution in the town, I did wonder what those poor Victorians were going to do now for entertainment every Christmas Eve, but I'm sure they got by, bless them.

However, none of this explains why you might be familiar with her name, and this is because that aspect of it came a couple of years later when the navy introduced tinned mutton rations for their sailors. The meat clearly could not have been all that appetising, as the seamen quickly suggested that the meat was, in fact, the butchered remains of sweet Fanny Adams that had finally been found after rotting away for a couple of years. This term quickly became associated with mediocre and substandard mutton and soon enough was being used to describe more or less anything that was considered worthless. The phrase then evolved into meaning time spent doing nothing at all, and men at the time pretended to their kids that Sweet F.A. actually stood for Sweet Fanny Adams rather than tell them that it was really Sweet Fuck All. Well, we couldn't have children using language like that, could we? Indeed, Sweet Fanny Adams is still used as a euphemism right up to this day, and thank goodness for that. I told you it was an interesting story, didn't I?

Her grave was incredibly neat and well kept, so someone was obviously taking the time to visit it regularly. Perhaps surviving relatives did the job, and a good job they were doing. The inscription was interesting and read as follows:

> *Sacred to the memory of Fanny Adams, aged 8 years and 4 months, who was cruelly murdered on Saturday, August 24th 1867. Fear not them which kill the body but are not able to kill the soul but rather fear Him which is able to destroy both body and soul in hell.*

On that happy note, we decided we had spent enough time here, but before we left Alton, we did have a walk to Flood Meadows, which we found at the end of the street where Fanny had lived. It was, as we should have probably expected, a lovely little park and looking around today, you would never guess that such a gruesome event occurred here all those years ago, although I'm sure all of the local people must know about it.

I got a lump in my throat when I saw a young family having a picnic under a tree near the river. Two little girls were playing football with their mum and dad, and I reckoned that they were probably about the same age as what poor Fanny Adams had been at the time of her murder. Although many years have passed and her death is just a bit of history to us, it suddenly struck me what a tragic and unimaginable time it must have been for everyone involved. It was not only time to leave Alton then, but it was time to cheer ourselves up, so we jumped back into the car to head for Herriard and the tale of the mad poet.

It was only a short ride, and just a few minutes later, we pulled up to park at possibly the poshest little car park I had ever seen, just off the main road. It was perhaps an old barn but had been converted into what looked like a rather long row of garages but without any doors. All of the bays were empty, so we claimed the middle one and went for a wander around the village, heading for the church we had just driven past.

As we got to the church, which was called St Mary's and is of some significance to our story, it appeared that some joker had turned the sign pointing to the church around, so it now pointed back to our car. They weren't going to get us that easily, though, I thought to myself as we crossed the road and was nearly run over by a Tesla. Damn electric cars, I thought to myself.

Herriard had been home to a gentleman, and I use that word generously, believe me, called George Puttenham, born here in 1529, who has gone down in history as a writer and literary critic. What he should, in fact, be known for is his raging insanity because the guy was clearly nuts for most of his life. He went to Cambridge to do a degree but never did one, yet was still somehow admitted to the English Bar, not a pub, of course, though he clearly spent most of his university days in one, but the type of Bar where you become a barrister. This is probably solely because he came from a wealthy background and is also the only reason nobody ever locked him up and threw away the key.

However, if they had, we would not have interesting stories to tell about him nowadays, so maybe we should think ourselves lucky. Anyway, he fell out with his brother-in-law, who he accused of stealing his pet goshawk of all things, and the two ended up fighting with daggers. This clearly did not impress his wife, Elizabeth, who divorced him shortly after, which we know from the vast wealth of court documents that survive detailing Puttenham as the nutjob that he was. He is variously described as a compulsive adulterer, a serial rapist, and a wife-beater, which helps to explain why Elizabeth wanted a divorce, in addition, of course, to the fact that Puttenham had tried to kill her little brother with a dagger.

Even before he was divorced from Elizabeth, he regularly had sex with his maids and impregnated at least one of them. To solve this tiny little problem, which we can presume did not make Elizabeth the happiest wife ever, he simply took the maid and the child on holiday to Belgium and cunningly left them there. After this, he had one of his servants travel down to London, kidnap a 17-year-old girl, and bring her back to the family home, where he raped her and kept her as a sex slave for several years. Puttenham gives the impression that he clearly thought he was above the law and that the rules didn't apply to him, but he was to come unstuck.

He somehow became implicated in a failed plot against a man called Lord Burghley, who was none other than the chief adviser to Queen Elizabeth I, and he was also accused of plotting to murder the Bishop of London. Even Puttenham couldn't get away with such antics, regardless of his background, and I chuckled to myself, imagining him asking *Do you know who I am?* as he was dragged off to prison. When the royal officials came to arrest him, however, the first attempt failed, as Puttenham had them tied up in this very churchyard and beaten around their heads, which cannot have helped his case, it has to be said.

This interesting story aside, we could find no sign

of a grave here, although we did not spend all that much time here, and as it was now time to move on, my thoughts turned to charging the car in Basingstoke which was just a short drive away.

I had never been to Basingstoke, and neither had Robin. I do know a couple of things about it from popular culture, though, such as when Rodney from Only Fools and Horses admitted to having once being busted for smoking a joint at Basingstoke Art College, which I don't think actually exists, by the way, and a probably much more famous example from The Hitchhiker's Guide to the Galaxy. In Douglas Adams' famous book, Arthur Dent is having difficulty getting his head around the idea that some aliens have just given them a lift in their spaceship, just like that, and he more or less asks if the aliens had offered to take them to the Basingstoke roundabout. It's amazing what you remember from your youth, but there you go. Other than that, my only impression of Basingstoke is that it has a reputation for being a boring little town.

We put the car on charge outside the very plush Village Hotel, and I decided that this was certainly the way to go for electric car charging. There was an abundance of chargers here, eight in total, and only one of them was already taken. It was almost a difficult decision choosing which one to use, so I looked at the one with the coolest name and chose Gwen-Jean, but only on the basis that I had relatives with both of those names, which I took as a good omen. They have names on them, by the way, only because it is easier to remember a name rather than a number, apparently.

I wandered into the hotel and asked the receptionist if I needed to pay for parking, explaining that we were not guests but would be happy to buy a drink or whatever in return for being allowed to charge the car there. She was very polite and said she would sort it and that there was no charge. Rather, she adamantly suggested that I did not have to buy a drink or anything else to charge either. She was maybe a bit too adamant, though, and I suspect that she just wanted my scruffy self out of the building, and I don't blame her one bit.

While the car was juicing up, Rob and I went for a walk to find the mythical Basingstoke roundabout. It was still incredibly hot, and although we did not see any spaceships, we soon found the roundabout though it was a little further away than expected. The roundabout had a name, and that was the Viables Roundabout. It is sort of famous as it is the only roundabout with its own light railway running on it, and this would be the Basingstoke and Alton Light Railway.

It was first built in 1901 and was actually the first-ever railway constructed by the Light Railway Commission, so it became pretty famous, at least for a while. As the name would suggest, it ran from Basingstoke to Alton and presumably back again, though it can't have had many trains at it was only a single-track railway.

During the First World War, the army borrowed it, digging it all up and taking it to France, where it became a military railway. They did swear a pinky-promise to bring it back after the war was over, but I imagine everyone was still pretty surprised when they actually delivered on their promise and brought it back and rebuilt it in 1924. It's probably a good thing that they did because did you know that the pinky-promise originated in Japan, and breaking one usually ended up with said finger being removed by something very sharp? I'm full of useless little snippets like that.

Anyway, this short piece of track before us is probably the shortest length of railway in the country at only a few feet long, and I mentioned to Rob that I was seriously considering whether or not the long walk had been worth it, suspecting that no, it was probably not. We needed a drink, and I just happened to know where we could get one, so off we popped to the Baverstock Arms pub.

After another fairly long walk, we found ourselves at the pub, but this is no ordinary pub. It is a museum within a museum and proved to be well worth the visit despite us paying to get in. From the outside, it is a modern, non-descript affair, but when you get in, it is a small but amazing capsule of days gone by. There's an old sweet shop, along with many other shops, some vintage vehicles – I particularly liked the fire engine, but they wouldn't let me have a go – all of which are all set around cobbled streets, and of course, there is a pub. We got talking to a guy called Greg on the way in, who said he was born and bred in Basingstoke, and who told us all about the museum we were about to explore. He also told us to visit Wote Street on the way back to the car. Although he didn't tell us why, he promised it would be worth it and that we would see the real Basingstoke, whatever that meant.

After a quick drink to refresh us and to wake us up a bit, we found some old arcade machines, and there was one that even promised to x-ray your feet for you. You might think that this is perhaps not a good idea, but years ago, they were very popular, and shoe shops worldwide had them so you could correctly size your feet. Their proper name was a pedoscope, and not much thought was given to their safety when they were introduced in the 1920s. In fact, it wasn't until after the Second World War and the dropping of two atomic bombs that people finally began to wonder if, on reflection, messing around with x-rays and radiation wasn't such a bright idea after all, yet still these machines continued in use until the 1970s. Switzerland was perhaps ahead of the game, banning them in 1959, yet even despite this ban, inspectors managed to find 160 of them in Zurich's shoe shops in 1960. My own dad had once told me a story of a time when he was younger, and he went to buy a pair of shoes and had seen one of these machines. Luckily, he never ended up using it because it cost so much money at the time, money that his mother never had. The machines were that bad that Time Magazine put them on its list of 100 Worst Inventions of the 20th century, alongside the likes of asbestos, the Titanic, and whoever promoted Kim Philby. Seriously.

We had not been in the museum too long, and we had certainly arrived late in the day, so it was Robin that noticed that some of the staff were staring at us, arms crossed, and looking at their watches. Figuring that they weren't hinting that we should ask them the time, we decided they wanted us to go home so that they could go home and that we were the only thing stopping them. It was then that we realised we were the only people left inside, so as we shuffled past them in shame, we apologised profusely and made our exit. They were very polite, but I still heard the door slam loudly behind us.

There was one last place on the list for Basingstoke, and as it was getting late, we decided to hurry it on, so we were pleased to find out that the Holy Ghost Cemetery, an odd name indeed for a cemetery, was actually directly between the Village Hotel and us, so we wouldn't even have to go out of our way.

When we got to the cemetery, we found that it was

still open and wandered up the winding road that led into it, passing beneath what looked like a fine footbridge. Unfortunately, there is no ghost, certainly not a holy one, and the name relates to the ruin that stands on the grounds.

That is not why we are here, though. We are here to see something that Robin was keen to come and look at, which is Mrs Alice Blunden's grave. I pondered whether this was the third or fourth grave today and decided third after Sir Alec Guinness and Fanny Adams, though for some reason, I thought there had been another.

Anyway, this story was still interesting in its way and slightly dark, but not anywhere near as gruesome as that of Fanny Adams. Alice had lived in Basingstoke with her husband William and evidently lived a very good life and was described as a *fat, gross woman*. One night, after consuming a rather large quantity of poppy water, and we should perhaps remember that poppies contain opium, Alice fell first into a deep sleep and then some kind of coma. A doctor was called when it became obvious that she could not be brought out of her state, and within a short time, she was declared dead.

Exactly like today, the day that Alice died had been a very hot one, so a quick burial was decided upon as no matter how much of a fat, gross woman poor Alice had been when she was alive, this was probably nothing on what she would become within a few hours on a hot, sunny, summer's day. It should be noted that obese humans, or obese anythings for that matter, decay much quicker than lean ones, which is something I neither knew nor had ever thought about, it should be said. So, in double-quick time, someone had dug a presumably big hole, at which point Alice was lowered into it inside her coffin, and that was the end of that.

Only it wasn't. A day later, some boys reported hearing haunting noises coming from down below while they had been playing in the cemetery, and although they were initially ignored, the authorities were forced to act when others reported exactly the same thing.

What they found was something that should only have come straight out of a nightmare. The coffin was beaten and broken, and Alice was covered in bruises and self-inflicted wounds, having presumably gone mad when she found herself in a somewhat sticky situation, to say the least. Three doctors examined her body once again and confidently declared her definitely dead this time, after which they should have waited for the coroner to inspect the body but decided not to. This was for the same reason as before, in that not only was Alice fat and gross, but in the heat of the day, she was about to become a lot more so. Instead, they decided to bury her once more and dig her up again when the coroner finally attended.

When the coroner dutifully reported the next day then, and when they had once again extracted poor Alice from her subterranean lodgings, those present were somewhat horrified to discover that Alice's injuries were now even worse than they had been the previous day and the damage to the inside of the coffin was even more so, suggesting that poor Alice had been buried alive not once, but twice.

Someone had to pay for this, of course, but who? A court case was brought, and the doctor's testimony cleared the family after he stated that he had administered the mirror test and that Alice had been unresponsive. Ultimately, the town was fined by Parliament for its negligence, which finally marked the end of this sorry episode. All that is left of this tale today is a blue plaque telling of this most miserable episode, which we found easily enough, though I wondered how much the actual fine was way back then for burying someone alive not once but twice.

As we headed back to the car, I figured there was no way we were going to get to our destination tonight, which was, of course, the pub, so after mentioning this to Rob, we decided to carry on with our little journey as there was still plenty of daylight left, and we were confident that we would come across a suitable little campsite somewhere along the way.

On a final note, we later found out that Thomas Burberry was buried in the Holy Ghost Cemetery, which was a shame as we could have gone to look for his grave had we known. I had no idea how he ended up here, but I thought it strange that we had come across him over breakfast in Hook, which now seemed a whole world away, having had such a busy day as we had.

So back to the car we went, via Wote Street, of course, wondering what delight was going to greet us there, and as we arrived at the end of the street, I think I can speak for the both of us when I say we were just a smidge disappointed. A typical drab high street greeted us, with an assortment of charity shops and chain stores, all topped off nicely with a McDonalds, and as we were just about to give up hope, we saw what we had come to see.

I hope you're not a prudish type of person because there standing proudly before us was a huge stone willy, right in the middle of the street stuck between a mobile phone shop and a barbershop. Apparently, it has been here for quite some time and is now affectionately known as the Woke Street Willy, which you have to admit is quite a catchy name.

It was erected, if you pardon the pun, in the mid-1990s and its proper name, so to speak, was the Church Stone, as this is the site of an old church. Quite why someone would want to commemorate an old church with a giant penis is completely beyond me, but what do I know? It was actually commissioned by the council, and their brief to the artist Michael Peglar was to bring peace to the place and reflect the town's history. I'm not sure what the ancient peoples of Basingstoke were previously known for, but one way or the other, they have now been paid tribute to with a huge stone schlong, bless them.

Indeed, at the unveiling, the sculpture attracted a certain amount of publicity, though not all of it was good. One local councillor even tried to have this mighty pecker taken away. However, thankfully here it still sits, presumably brightening up the day of many surprised shoppers and passers-by. Unfortunately, we were the only passers-by paying any attention to this thing today, and this is when it dawned on me that this might look a trifle odd, so I decided to give the thing a hug while Rob took a photo of me. Well, in for a penny, in for a pound.

Quite bizarrely, the artist said that he just didn't see it as a phallic symbol, which is odd when that is exactly what it is, but he was a good sport and thought that the nickname the thing had attracted was, and I quote, rather nice. Another person who thought it rather nice was Sarah Brightman, who just happened to be performing at the Haymarket Theatre when it was unveiled. When she heard about it, she was reported to have said, and I'm going to quote once again, she said *it's beautiful, as soon as I saw it, I just wanted to touch it.* Enough said.

We finally got back to the car a little later than

anticipated and decided that we had better hit the road and get out of town. It had been a really long day, and we had managed to visit many interesting places, but our thoughts turned to finding somewhere to sleep for the night. I imagined there were not many campsites within Basingstoke, so as the sun hung low over this interesting and not at all boring little town, we drove straight into the sunset, just like in the movies.

We were heading towards the North Wessex Downs, and specifically the village of Hannington. We had heard that the village pub, The Vine, is a popular spot for hikers walking the Wayfarer's Walk, and they were partial to letting people camp in the beer garden in exchange for buying a pint or two. After what seemed like an incredibly long ride, though was in fact just half a dozen miles or so, we had pulled up in the car park, spoken to the young lady behind the bar, pitched our tent, and were now sat supping a nice cold pint in the cool interior of the pub. It's amazing how quickly you can get stuff done when there is a bit of an incentive, Rob winked to me as he supped the froth off of his beer.

We reflected on the day's journey, still quite amazed and quite frankly pretty pleased with ourselves that we had managed to cover so many miles and had seen so many places today, as this is exactly what we had imagined the trip to be like. Charging the car had not been particularly problematic today, and all in all, today had been a breeze.

Stopping at this pub had been a double bonus as well because as we looked through the menu, it seemed as if the gods were shining upon us. I chose their house beef burger, topped with caramelised onions and stilton, while Robin went for minted Barnsley lamb, and as usual, when the food arrived, I found myself rather jealous and wished that I too had ordered the lamb. Another pint washed it all down, and it was relatively late when we found ourselves drifting merrily off to sleep in our tents, though this time we were not afraid of being discovered by an irate farmer or squashed at some point with a tractor. That night I dreamed of Basingstoke.

WHITE HORSES EVERYWHERE

Today would be a good day, we decided, with lots of interesting places to visit that neither of us had been to before. We were up at the crack of dawn once again, and once again, Rob was playing chef while I dried out the tents, which was easy in the strong morning sunshine even at this early hour. We tried to be as quiet as possible, thinking that all sensible people were still in bed, and by the time we had had our coffee and eaten and were pulling the car out of the car park, we had still not seen or heard another soul. The good thing about electric cars is that you can always make your escape in absolute silence, of course, so I'm pretty sure that we didn't disturb anybody despite being on the road for not much after 5am.

We drove first to Kingsclere, a minor stop, and pulled up at the church. Sitting proudly atop the tower of St Mary's was a rather unusual weather vane, in the form of a bed bug, of all things. While you might imagine that this is definitely a trifle odd and perhaps not something to be proud of, there is a short but interesting story behind this, which goes as follows.

Sometime in the 13th century, while King John travelled through the area, bad weather forced him to make an unscheduled stop on his journey. Finding himself in Kingsclere, with some versions of the story saying he spent the night in a pub while another says he spent it with some monks, the king enjoyed a rather uncomfortable night, and as a consequence, ordered the erection of the bed bug weather vane so that his ordeal should never be forgotten by the villagers, shame on them. Whether this story is true or not is debatable, as bed bugs did not become widespread in the UK until around the 1930s, which saw the introduction of heating systems in our homes. Others say the bed bug isn't a bed bug at all but is, in fact, a tortoise, but I have never seen a six-legged tortoise, have you?

We jumped back into the car and sped next to a place of myth, one that I had never considered was real, and that was Watership Down. Made famous by the 1978 movie of the real name, I remember going to see this film as a mere whippersnapper, and I also remember that it was incredibly sad, leaving me in floods of tears and wondering what had gone through my parents' minds by taking me to see what was essentially, for a six-year-old at least, a horror movie.

Anyway, we parked at the White Hill car park and slowly began our early morning climb up the hill.

The sky was a glory of colour, and as we made our way up, the sun rose gently behind us, warming our backs. We had hoped to see rabbits and were not disappointed, so it was easy to see where Richard Adams got his inspiration for the book that became the film that so upset my younger self. I'm happy to report that none of the rabbits we saw today died, but they all scurried away when they saw us for some reason.

We walked up to the top of the hill and found a trig point, which offered spectacular views in all directions and was a treat we enjoyed purely for us. There was still clearly no one else awake in the whole of Hampshire, apparently, but as we walked back down to the car, we were finally able to talk to someone else who had managed to escape from their slumber, and that was Vera.

Vera was a weathered dog walker who looked as if she had spent the entirety of her obviously long life outdoors and had acquired a deep veneer to her skin as a result. Shep, her rather unimaginatively named dog, bounded around as we talked about this and that, clearly trying to snap up a rabbit for his breakfast, though every time he approached one, they darted into one dark hole or another hidden in the grass.

We explained what we were doing in trying to travel in an electric car straight up the middle of the country, avoiding all the rivers, and she seemed to be genuinely interested and asked us if we had heard of Oswald Mosley, which of course we had. He had spent the entire war under house arrest at nearby Crux Easton, she told us and added that we should visit the place to look at the wind engine, whatever that was. She added that if we were going to Crux Easton, then we might as well pop to Ashmansworth, which had been the home of George Bissill, which is not a name that I am familiar with. When I asked her who he was, she told me to look it up, bade us farewell, and went on her way with her dog.

I looked at Rob, who looked at me, and as we shrugged our shoulders, we thought we had no choice but to do as she said. What could possibly go wrong?

Crux Easton looked to be the nearest of the two villages, so as Rob looked at the map, I took us down a series of country roads, passing the busy A34 and rolling into the village a short while later. The wind engine was pretty easy to find, being basically a rather tall windmill, though it did not look like a traditional windmill. It more resembles one that you would imagine are dotted around the mid-west of America if you know what I mean, but it was nonetheless quite pleasing to the eye. Our chances of actually getting a closer look were slim, as a sign said that the site was only open on the second Sunday of each month from 11am until 4pm, which you must admit is a somewhat limited time frame. Undaunted, we hopped the fence anyway, being the rebels that we are, and found another sign that said the engine had been built for Lord Carnarvon and was originally used for pumping water out of the ground.

We went off to find Oswald Mosley's house and assuming we found the right one, which I think we did, it was just behind the wind engine. It was a small house and pleasant enough and is where Oswald Mosley spent the latter part of his internment during the Second World War.

If you have not heard of Oswald Mosley, it is fair to say that he was a dangerous man. Born into a wealthy family, he attended Sandhurst Military College but was thrown out for fighting. He transferred to the Royal Flying Corps but managed to crash a plane while showing off to his mother and sister, though he did fight in the trenches at the Battle of Loos in 1915. Much later, during the 1930s, he spent his time prancing around Italy, quite literally, having been mesmerised by Mussolini, who was, of course, the fascist dictator of the country and a good chum of Hitler.

Mosley came back to Britain and thought he would take our little island in the same direction, forming the British Union of Fascists in 1932. This is perhaps odd, as earlier in his life, Mosley had been influenced by Gandhi, renowned peace lover, in India.

Anyway, at the outset of the war, the secret service

kept close tabs on Mosley, and as soon as Churchill came to power in 1940, Mosley was marched off to Holloway Prison, where he was kept until 1943. As the tide of war was then judged to be turning in favour of the allies, everyone calmed down a bit when it came to Mosley, and it was decided that he could, in fact, go home, so long as he promised to be a good boy. So, it is here that he spent the rest of the war under house arrest, and that was the end of that.

As I said, it is a nice house indeed, and I could not imagine a nicer prison. It was a bit early to knock on the door and ask for a guided tour, though, so we wandered back down to the small church just to have a look, really. The door was open, and as we wandered in, I was startled to hear a voice from inside wish us good morning and found an elderly gentleman mopping the floor. This was George, and he lived locally and was incredibly friendly indeed. In no time at all, he had told us his entire life story and was asking us about ours, so we told him what we were doing and where we were going. He told us that we simply had to have a look at the wind engine before we went, even though I had just told him that we had already been up there, and he also told us that Charles de Havilland was once the vicar here, though I had no idea who he was on about as this name meant nothing to me. Rob and I got the impression that we could have been here all day, and part of us would have loved to stay, but we said our goodbyes to George and went back to the car.

We knew full well where we were going next, and this was Highclere Castle. If you ever visit the castle, it might look quite familiar, for it is here that much of Downton Abbey was filmed. Never a fan myself, my mother-in-law banned us all from visiting while this was on, which was fine by me, and I just wish it was on more often, to be honest.

The place has a long and illustrious history, and I could go on and on about it, and I promise I won't, but there are at least a few things that simply have to be said about it. For instance, it is here that Lorn Carnarvon lived, although his real name was the much less impressive George Herbert. This is, of course, the gentleman that financed the search and ultimately the excavation of Tutankhamun's tomb in the Egyptian Valley of the Kings, which was officially opened on February 16th 1923, by Howard Carter. The castle ultimately became home to many of the artefacts recovered by Carter, the archaeologist that the Lord employed, events which, of course, became famous due to the so-called curse of the pharaohs that followed the opening of the tomb.

Indeed, Lord Carnarvon himself was said to have become the first victim of the curse. He was bitten by a mosquito, so the story goes, and later managed to slice into the bite wound while shaving. This, in turn, became infected, which resulted in blood poisoning, and the Lord promptly dropped down dead on April 5th 1923, less than two months after the official opening of the tomb.

When an autopsy was later carried out on Tutankhamun's mummified remains, he was found to have a lesion on his cheek that was said to be in the same place as Lord Carnarvon's ultimately fatal mosquito bite, which, you have to admit, is a bit creepy.

Sir Arthur Conan Doyle, obviously taking a break from writing his blockbuster Sherlock Holmes novels, added fuel to the fire when he suggested that Carnarvon's death was linked to the supernatural, which caused a media frenzy further compounded by other deaths soon after. Over the years, several others succumbed to the curse. The final alleged death which was put down, by some at least, to the curse of the pharaohs was that of Howard Carter himself. However, it has to be said that this was in 1939, and he died after a long battle with cancer.

We had parked up in the village of Highclere even before the Castle had opened, but we had a cunning plan. Not wanting to pay to go and see something that we would only spend a few minutes looking at, we had instead found out that there are public footpaths that run through the grounds, and which would give us a good view of the house, so we were soon wandering through the beautiful gardens that make up the estate, and we did not deviate from the public footpath once, I swear to God on a pinky-promise. While I would perhaps like to come back one day and have a proper look around, I must say that the public footpath offered as good a view of the house as anyone would want, while at the same time being absolutely free.

There are two more things I want to say about the place, and then we shall move on, I promise, but I did tell you it was full of history. Anyway, Canada was created at Highclere Castle, with the document that founded the country being signed here, way back in the 1860s, which was the British North America Act in case you're interested, and to celebrate this wonderful creation of a more polite version of America, someone planted a maple tree in the grounds a few years back.

And lastly, very lastly, I promise, Highclere is where you can find some excellent examples of the Cedar Tree of Lebanon, which were collected and brought here for planting by a man called Bishop Pococke after he visited the middle east in the 1700s. Rather strangely, a Reverend Edward Pococke, one time vicar of nearby Chieveley, also visited Lebanon in search of the exact same seeds sometime earlier, although they neither knew of each other, were not aware of the other's existence, did not seem to be related and lived at different times.

Luckily, both Rob and I love walking, so we continued along the paths all the way to Beacon Hill, where we found the grave of Lord Carnarvon himself. The tomb was contained within an iron fence and occupied a beautiful spot on the hill, and was also the site of an ancient iron age hill fort. I noticed that the plaque gave his name as George Edward Stanhope Molyneaux and missed out on the Herbert. I mused that this was a posh person thing and that Molyneaux was somehow preferential to Herbert. While Lord Carnarvon will endure all eternity in this beautiful setting, Carter was buried in obscurity in Putney, West London, where his grave quickly became neglected, though efforts have recently been made to restore it.

As we left, and as we were mooching around the site, Robin stumbled across a stone that told us this had been the site where Geoffrey de Havilland had attempted his first flight in his homemade aeroplane on September 10, 1910, and I immediately remembered that George had told us that Charles de Havilland had been the vicar at nearby Crux Easton. It turns out that Charles was Geoffrey's dad, so there you go, that was one mystery solved.

It is important to say that the stone doesn't tell the full story, however. While Geoffrey took off from here, he never landed as such, although technically, you could describe a crash landing as a landing, though most wouldn't. His plane was wrecked, and he had to build another one, which he flew from nearby Newbury and which was a bit more successful. As we were discussing this, Rob reminded me of the old adage that any landing you can walk away from is a good landing, and he had a point, I guess.

Anyway, de Havilland proved to be pretty good at building stuff that could fly, and within a few years, he set up what eventually became one of the largest aircraft companies in the country and even the world, producing such wonders as the Tiger Moth, the Mosquito, and after the Second World War, the Comet. The Tiger Moth and the Mosquito were great and probably helped save the country from the Germans, but the Comet was, well, not so great and had a nasty habit of falling from the sky, which, let's face it, could really spoil your day. Apparently, the problem was the square windows, which tended to pop out, and when they were re-designed to be round, it more or less solved the problem, though the damage was already done. In another unfortunate incident, the company wanted to show off its new fighter at the 1952 Farnborough air show just up the road, though it crashed into a crowd of spectators, killing several people. Amazingly, on the day, the organisers, in true British spirit, simply cleared the debris and bodies out of the way and carried on with the air-show. Anyway, Hawker Siddeley eventually took over De Havilland, which then dabbled in things like the Blue Streak, an experimental missile cum space rocket, but that also tended to crash, so all in all, there was at least a link between the old and new company.

We were now back at the car, and jumping in, we were heading west. There was, however, just one teeny, tiny problem. The car didn't work.

I pressed the button to start it and had my foot on the brake as you should, and although the car made a funny noise, which was a really short beep, nothing happened. The dashboard remained dark, and there was no sign of life, so after a few minutes of scratching my chin and making funny shapes with my mouth, which I am very good at, by the way, I did the only thing I could think of and called our breakdown service.

All credit to them, they were on site after just twenty minutes. The technician, who introduced himself as Mark though I suspect this was not his real name as he then changed it to Mike, diagnosed the problem in no time at all, although he clearly sighed when he saw that he was dealing with an electric car and a pair of chimps who had no idea what they were doing. He had a big bushy beard and was around five feet wide and looked like he would be at home in the special forces, I thought to myself as he poked around under the bonnet with a strange but small machine. Basically, he told us that the car had been subject to having being operated by a couple of idiots, who had failed to turn the ignition off when we had parked it up, which had then drained the battery, and that we were lucky nobody had decided to drive off in the thing, not that they would have got far in it, he remarked.

He didn't mean the big battery, by the way, but the accessory battery that makes sure the car starts and is much the same, in fact exactly the same, as a twelve-volt battery on any car. He then took out some cables, connected various things to various other things, and told us to wait just a jiffy. After a few minutes, he disconnected everything again without managing to electrocute anybody, which is always a bonus, and promptly started the car.

He then gave us a little tip, which was to put the windscreen wipers on for the next mile or two, as for some reason, these little electric Leafs charge the accessory battery when the wipers are operating, he advised. I thought he was kidding, but he assured us he doesn't kid, and we believed him, and I wondered how many people he had killed in his last job. By now, his name had changed to Matt, and as he put his sunglasses back on and hoisted his rifle over his right shoulder, he told us in a friendly but vaguely threatening manner not to make the same mistake twice, and then he drove off.

The Leaf has a little solar panel on the back, which is supposed to keep the twelve-volt battery topped up, but due to the early hour and because we had stupidly parked the car under a tree and made sure to point it north, the panel had little effect. As we headed out of Highclere, with the windscreen wipers squeaking out a noisy protest on the dry and dusty windscreen, I felt a bit of a twit, it has to be said. When I next parked the car, I told myself I would make sure it was not under a tree, was facing south, and I definitely positively would make sure I turned the thing off properly. As we drove, Rob and I discussed Matt, or Mike, or whoever he was. We decided that he was indeed ex-SAS or something similar and also decided that he was quite handy with cars.

Presently, we found ourselves at a Tesco in Marlborough, where we once again plugged the car in to charge. I presumed that it would also charge the twelve-volt battery up by plugging it in now, so we left it there in the sun and walked down the hill and into town to find some food.

It was late morning and very hot, and soon enough, we found a chip shop where we both bought ourselves a greasy lunch. We poured on a healthy and generous portion of salt and vinegar and wandered through the town eating it, heading towards Marlborough College. Marlborough is not a big place, and after following the River Og for a while, which we both agreed was a most excellent name for a river, we were soon at the college and looking for a pile of earth.

I say a pile of earth, but it was technically a mound that we wanted to see, for this is the last resting place of none other than Merlin, famous wizard to King Arthur and up until Harry Potter, the most famous wizard in the wizarding world, probably. We found it soon enough, and I was surprised to find it bigger than I had expected. It has previously been described as Silbury's little sister, in reference to nearby Silbury Hill, which is supposed to be the largest prehistoric hill in Europe, and was until relatively recently thought to date from Norman times, believe it or not. Recent research has suggested that this smaller hill might actually be prehistoric too, which unfortunately means that Merlin is probably not beneath it, and we have walked all the way here for absolutely nothing. Still, it gave the car the chance to charge.

The day was getting on, so we decided to pull our socks up and have an afternoon of short sharp visits to the various places that were on our way. We now had a fully charged car, and as we left Marlborough, heading south, we immediately got stuck behind not one, but four, combine harvesters. We were about three cars behind and not particularly bothered about travelling at such a slow speed as we now found ourselves going, for two reasons. Firstly, we were on holiday, and although I had told my wife that this was a research trip for this book, it was definitely a holiday. She will never read it, so I have nothing to worry about, and Robin promised not to tell either. Secondly, if you remember from the beginning, the slower an electric car travels, the greater its range will be. There is an incredibly complicated explanation for this, but I don't understand it fully, so I am just going to say it is something to do with physics, and you will have to take my word for it.

Anyway, we slowly trundled along, and it seemed that the farmers in front of us were all on their annual day out and were going to see the Pewsey White Horse, which by some amazing and unlikely coincidence, was exactly where we were going.

I was wrong, however, and the farmers all turned off towards Wilcott while we continued on to the horse. When the satnav told us that we had arrived at our destination, I slammed the brakes on and brought the car to a halt, apparently in the middle of nowhere and with no horse in sight. It dawned on us then that we would have perhaps had a better view of the horse had we parked a mile or so to the north, rather than drive right up to it as we had done, but we were here now, and being the stubborn old fools that we were, we dumped the car on a grass verge and set off on foot instead.

We were on a high hill, and the views were absolutely spanking in all areas apart from one – there wasn't a horse to be seen. We hopped over a stile and walked a few yards, and as we were almost about to give up on finding the beast, we realised we were stood right on top of it. A gate took us into a small enclosed field, where we could really appreciate the horse up close, and also so we could get a photo or two, which is when I had a cunning plan. I asked Robin if he wanted a photo of him with the horse, knowing full well that he would say yes, and then took his camera and positioned him accordingly. What he didn't know at the time was that I made him stand right on top of where the horse's penis would be, made sure he was at just the right angle and took my photo. With his bald head, I'm sure I don't need to tell you exactly what he looked like, and I can't wait until he reads this, if he ever does, and goes back for a second look at the photos. I had previously read that the people that maintain this horse had described it as a *'well-proportioned representation of the real animal'*, and they were not wrong, though it was made only better with the addition of my good friend Rob, I must say.

We had both become really excited about seeing a white horse, so to treat ourselves, we decided to go and look at another one straight away. This next one was the Alton Barnes White Horse, and within fifteen minutes and after having been stuck behind exactly zero combine harvesters, we were pulling into the small car park where we found just one free space, which was all we needed.

It was only a two-minute walk to the horse, which appeared to be larger than the one at Pewsey, although we knew it would be because Pewsey is the smallest of the lot. It also looked very similar in form, possibly because it was probably designed by the same person responsible for the Pewsey Horse, a man going by the name of Robert Pile. As we walked along the edge of the hill for a while to get a better view, as again we were too close, I told Rob the amusing story of how this one came to be.

In 1812, Mr Pile paid a painter going by the dubious name of Jack the Painter, the princely sum of £20 to personally cut the horse for him, and we should remember that this was a lot of money at the time. Jack, who wasn't called Jack at all but was really called John Thorne, had no intention of cutting the horse himself but instead subcontracted the job to a third gentleman also and confusingly called John, specifically John Harvey. Harvey was perhaps more honest than Thorne and started work on the job without an advance of cash, which was perhaps not the best idea he ever had. Once Harvey had finished cutting the horse, Thorne ran away with the money and was never seen again, at least not in these parts. It is thought that Robert Pile then had to pay John Harvey yet another twenty pounds to finish the job properly, which he clearly did, and a fine job he did indeed as it still looks very good today. Thorne never did pay the money back, but with a hint of karma, he was later arrested and executed for an unrelated crime.

There is another white horse nearby, just north of Devizes, called the Cherhill White Horse. We're going to give that one a miss, though, as we really don't see the need to stop at yet another one, although we did see it from the road on our way to Compton Bassett later on. It was cut in 1870, much later than the other two, and was quite happily minding its own business until it came into the 21st century. For some reason, some idiot covered the horse in black stripes in 2005 to give it more of an exotic appearance and make it look like a panda. Those responsible owned the local FIAT car franchise and had hoped to promote their new car of the same name.

Now, I don't know about you, but I imagine that you could paint as many black stripes on a horse as you want, but it will never look like a panda. Not surprisingly, therefore, their publicity stunt was derided everywhere and even made the national news. Even though it looked like a zebra, however, their little stunt certainly did the trick regarding free publicity, which was perhaps what they had intended all along?

A white horse that we were going to stop at was just to the north of Devizes, another little gem of a place that I had never had the pleasure of visiting. We parked on the outskirts of the town and took the short walk to the horse, or more accurately, to the place where we could best view the horse from. There seemed little point in walking up the hill to the horse itself, and it looked far better from half a mile away anyway, so we simply admired it from afar.

We didn't spend long here, as to be honest, we had seen more than our fair share of horses today, and there isn't a lot to say about this particular one. Although it is believed an older white horse once stood in or very near to this spot, it was not ancient, but this one was constructed to mark the new millennium just a few years ago. I had always associated white horses with crop circles and UFOs, both of which were sadly lacking in this area today, but had a UFO appeared, or even a crop circle, we might have stuck around.

As it was, we ventured back to the car, passing close to a small village called Roundway, which is a tiny place with not a lot to say for itself. There was a battle here during the civil war, which the Royalists won, and a nearby hill was mistakenly named Olivers Fort on the basis that Oliver Cromwell fought in the battle, but this is a load of tosh, and he never set foot near here.

Devizes has a lot to say for itself, on the other hand, but not all of it is good. One of the juiciest things I could find about it was that this town was once home to Rebecca Smith, who lived and died here in the 1800s. She was actually the last woman to be executed for infanticide in the UK. It is said that of her eleven children, she killed eight of them with poison. Only her firstborn survived, with the other two dying of natural causes. She was hanged in the town in 1849.

What Devizes distinctly lacked nowadays, however, was electric car chargers, though luckily we had plenty of miles left yet on the old Leaf. Rob studied the map and promptly directed us north, ignoring a sign that led south to Salisbury, which is both a very nice place and has recently become popular with Russian tourists, apparently.

We went through Calstone Wellington without stopping, not because it sounds like some kind of stew, but because there was little to see here. Its one claim to fame is that it is the home of Britain's oldest road apparently, although it seemed to be in far superior condition to many of the roads in my home town of Hull, where the local council have systematically decided to destroy whatever roads we have and install a mysterious network of cycle lanes at great expense to us all, but which are seldom used. This place is right on the watershed line, though, and is the source of the River Marden, which flows first to the Avon and then into the Bristol Channel and the Atlantic Ocean. Theoretically, then, you could pop a little rubber ducky into the water here and then just fly to the Bahamas and, well, wait.

It was shortly after this that we saw the Cherhill White Horse, but as I mentioned earlier, we had no intention of stopping, but we didn't need to anyway, as we had a fine view from the road. Unfortunately, it was the wrong road, and after a quick turnaround, we were once again heading for Langley Burrell, though we made a quick pit-stop at Compton Bassett.

Parking outside the beautiful White Horse Inn, the perfect name of course for a pub in these parts, we wandered down a leafy lane through the village, passing some very nice houses indeed. St Swithin's Church was at the other end of the village, though it was still only a short walk, and we were soon passing through the door and into the church itself. The place was beautifully carved with a fine stained-glass window, and while it was all very nice, there was another reason why we wanted to visit the place, and that was because this was the site of one of the most notorious crimes ever to have occurred in Compton Bassett, which is probably not that many when you think about it.

Anyway, a few years ago, a 65-year-old lady called Midge Mather broke into the pretty 12th-century church after losing her patience with the sound of the church bells, which she clearly found rather annoying. This little old lady, first of all, smashed her way in through the not inconsiderable door using an axe, a crowbar and a hack-saw, which must have been quite a sight in itself. I would have happily pulled up a chair, grabbed a drink and some popcorn, and sat to watch this event for pure entertainment value alone, but maybe that's just me. It gets better, though. Once inside, she systematically cut through the bell ropes, which took her almost two hours in a concerted and premeditated effort to silence them forevermore.

She probably would have gotten away with it, too, apart from one small detail. Quite bizarrely, when she got home, she picked up her telephone, called the local police station, and made a full and immediate confession. She had previously warned the Archdeacon of Wiltshire of her intentions, but I reckon even he must have been surprised when she actually carried out her audacious plan. She more or less got away with it anyway, receiving just a conditional discharge, but she even kicked off at that, so she was taken down to the cells to cool off for a bit. I'm not sure about you, but I know exactly where I stand on this. If you move into a nice little cottage next to a church that has been there for eight hundred years, don't complain about the bells. On a final note, it is definitely worth noting that Midge was named after something rather annoying herself, which is perhaps rather fitting.

We didn't stay long, as although Compton Bassett is a really nice place, there is little to see. This is perhaps why Michael Mcintyre and Robbie Williams had previously chosen to live in these parts, and we had hoped to bump into them, but we never did, so off we trundled to our next place on the list. We had hoped to pop to New Zealand on the way, not the country of course but a village of the same name, and also to Clyffe Pypard, where there used to be an airfield that flew the De Havilland Tiger Moth, but due to Robin's continued confusion as to which way left actually was, we completely missed them out and decided that we would use up too much range retracing our steps.

We had also briefly considered a diversion to

Swindon to grab a quick charge but decided not to for three reasons. First, it was actually quite a bit out of the way, and we wanted to crack on, although if we had chosen to go to either New Zealand or Clyffe Pypard, it would have made sense. Second, I had previously had a bit of a near-death experience in Swindon, which I was keen not to repeat. This had been almost two full years ago and would have had me in the same place on almost the exact same day, which I took to be both a prophecy and a warning. I had been passing through the town on the way to Salisbury and had somehow ended up on what I considered at the time to be possibly the worst designed junction I had ever laid my eyes on. As I pulled up to it, I realised I was at a mini-roundabout, but another roundabout was directly in front of me, though this one was much larger. I tried to process this for a minute, which would have been fine and was, in fact, going pretty well, until I realised that there was yet another mini roundabout to my left and another to my right, at which point I nearly had a stroke.

I had had my foot firmly on the brake at the time and had become dimly aware somewhere in my subconsciousness of flashing lights and some strange buzzing. This actually turned out to be the flashing headlights and blaring horn of the driver behind me, who probably rightly wondered what the hell I was doing and for how long exactly I planned to live at this roundabout.

Obviously, at times like this, the pressure is on, and as I checked to see if the way was clear, I figured it was. Now usually, in this country at least, traffic goes around roundabouts in a clockwise direction. For some reason, and this is something I only noticed as I pulled away and directly into its path, a truck was going around the larger roundabout anti-clockwise. I was in my wife's car at the time, which is diesel, by the way, so as I pressed my foot hard on the accelerator, two things happened simultaneously. Firstly, the car blew out a big cloud of diesel smoke, and secondly, it wholly failed to accelerate any faster, as diesel cars are often apt to do.

I have no idea how the truck never hit me, though I think it just about removed a millimetre of paint from the rear bumper, so close did we pass. Escaping the roundabout completely, I pulled up so that I could restart my heart with a defibrillator and to see what the hell was going on with the idiot in the truck, who had skidded to a halt on one of the smaller roundabouts and who had evidently stalled his vehicle which now appeared to be reluctant to restart.

It appears, however, that I was the idiot because the truck driver had, in fact, been following the correct protocol, which compels motorists to drive around the mini-roundabouts in the usual clockwise direction, though directs them anti-clockwise around the big one. I tried to read up on this crazy junction later and discovered that it was called the magic roundabout, named directly after the children's series of the same name that had been written by some drugged-up hippies in the 1970s. I could only guess that similar lifestyles had surrounded the designers of this monstrosity. Just to give you an idea of what I mean, the cartoon featured a sleepy rabbit who constantly plays the guitar, a cow called Ermintrude who constantly appears to eat something that looks like poppies, and, my own personal favourite, a shaggy dog, called Dougal who develops an addiction to *'sweets'* and is soon on two bags a day. I grew up with this programme and loved it, but don't read anything into that, will you? Lastly, it's no coincidence that this roundabout opened in 1972, exactly at the height of the TV programme, and although I couldn't remember the third reason for not wishing to visit Swindon, surely the other two are more than enough?

Anyway, back to our journey. We were specifically heading for St Peter's Church in Langley Burrell by now, where we were going to pay tribute to someone that we had both grown up with and that someone was Norris McWhirter. He was, of course, famous for the television show Record Breakers, but he was also a keen athlete himself, which is presumably how he became interested in world records. I can fondly remember getting a copy of the Guinness Book of Records for Christmas every year when I was younger, and I have also bought my children a copy on occasion, as it is quite simply a rite of passage for any kid to own a copy at some time in their childhood. I had always intended to break a world record myself, though I never managed to do so and to be honest, I'm not sure exactly what I could be capable of.

It's not over yet, though, and I reckon I could be in the running for some of the more obscure records out there, such as most Big Macs consumed in a lifetime, which I must surely at least have a fighting chance at, or maybe world's biggest mouth, a distinct possibility according to my wife, or if I start work now, I could build the world's largest hat in around five-years, though it would have to be bigger than the current record of 15 feet and nine inches tall. Who knows?

Anyway, we found his grave and duly paid our respects before having a quick look in the church and then moving on. We had a very important mission next, which was to drive a few more miles west to a village, although I cannot yet give you the name of where we were heading. As we pulled up, though, we took out our props, which were some small, round plastic discs, and in front of a sign that said *Tiddleywink Please Drive Carefully*, we played the game of the same name. As a local dog walker came along and gave us a bit of a funny look, I suggested that she probably saw this sort of thing all the time, grown men playing tiddlywinks in front of the village sign. She replied that she certainly had never seen anything of the such ever before and walked off clearly somewhat perplexed. I do love the fact that whenever we are somewhere doing something stupid, which is almost everywhere and most of the time in mine and Rob's case, there is usually someone who is just lucky enough to witness our various antics, and I often wonder what on earth they must think of us?

This was really just a photo opportunity, and soon enough, we were back in the car and heading towards Chippenham, where we intended to get a charge of the fast type. We had been watching our miles tick off slowly today and now only had enough left to get us into town, although there were several chargers to choose from, so we did not anticipate problems. Unfortunately, and completely of my own doing, and I really cannot blame Rob for this, a series of wrong turns soon had us going in completely the wrong direction, and by some perfect storm of bad luck and sheer stupidity, I somehow managed to get us onto the motorway heading for Bristol, which was neither intended nor useful in any way whatsoever.

Now I'm not sure about you, but when I find myself under pressure, I sometimes make the wrong decisions, which is exactly what I did next, as when we got to the next junction, I turned the car around and headed straight back towards

Chippenham, without ever considering how many miles away it was or how many miles the car had left in the battery.

Unfortunately, the former was more than the latter, so it was a good two miles short of the exit junction that the Leaf reported it had zero miles left, which was clearly a problem, although I did notice that it went from four to zero in one go, and missed out three, two and one. I sincerely hoped that this meant that the car was trying to trick me into finding a charger by telling me there were no miles left, when in fact, there were four, but this was clearly wishful thinking on my part.

By some miracle, we escaped the motorway and certain death and turned south towards the town. A not-helpful sign told us there was still four miles to go, and as we passed the sign, something appeared on the dashboard that I had never seen before. I had long heard rumours of and even had nightmares about this something – which was, of course, that small yellow tortoise. I had heard it also described as a turtle, but as they live in the water and are presumably pretty quick, and a tortoise lives on the land and is a bit slower, I'm sticking with tortoise.

Anyway, the tortoise appeared, and the car immediately slowed to around thirty miles per hour, which was a problem as the rest of the traffic wanted to do around fifty, so I had no choice but to pull off the road immediately. I thought I had pulled onto a side road, but unfortunately, I realised I had pulled into the driveway of someone's house or possibly a farm. Anyway, wherever we were, we had no choice but to stop, and this meant only one thing – calling the breakdown service for the second time in one day.

I had no phone signal, though, but I did seem to be able to get a slow internet connection, and after a surprisingly small number of button presses, I was informed that a driver would be with me in forty minutes.

We sat there in the late afternoon sun, praying that the property owner would not come home at this most inopportune moment, and thankfully the only vehicle that turned up was our trusty breakdown truck.

The driver swung into the lane and pulled up behind us, and as we jumped out, we realised it was the same one from this morning, though he had probably changed his name to Bob or something else by now.

Surprisingly, he was very polite and friendly and seemed to be laughing at us out of pity more than anger. I apologised and said how sorry I was for wasting his time, to which he replied that it was idiots like us that kept him in his job, and I guessed he had a point. Of course, he was much more polite than to actually use those particular words, but I know what he meant.

He asked me if I had managed to drain the twelve-volt battery again, to which I proudly replied no, instantly realising that what I had actually done was far, far worse. When I told him that I had managed to drain the traction battery, for that is what it is called, you see, he simply burst out laughing and got back in his truck.

I feared he would leave us there to die in the night or be picked off one by one in the morning by the locals, but instead, he moved his truck in front of the car, clearly preparing to give us a lift.

He was an expert at what he did, and it took him no time at all to get us onto the back of the truck, which was fortunate as a khaki-clad farmer had now rolled up in his Land Rover and discovered he was going to have to wait for his cup of tea a little while longer after all.

Within thirty minutes, however, we found ourselves deposited at a rapid charger in the centre of Chippenham, and as soon as Marco or whatever his name was had confirmed that the car was actually charging, he jumped back into his cab and started the engine. Leaning out of his open window, he told us that he never wanted to see us again and that if he did, he was going to bury us in the woods where nobody would ever find us. He actually said to have a safe journey and make sure we get a charge in plenty of time, but once again, we knew exactly what he meant.

It was getting a bit late now, so once again, our thoughts turned to thinking about where we were going to stay for the night. We really wanted a proper campsite as the both of us desperately needed a shower, and after consulting our trusty map, we found one just outside of Malmesbury, so we decided to hit the town first and then head for the campsite.

There was a charger in the town that was listed on Zapmap. Still, when we arrived at its location, we were greeted with a level of security that suggested experiments to build a new type of nuclear missile or something else extremely secret. A stern-looking security guard, possibly related to the private contractor that had been the breakdown man, approached the car and told us in no uncertain terms to stop.

This was actually the top-secret, hi-tech Dyson factory that built, well, vacuum cleaners, amongst other things. The car was still pretty charged up, so this was not a major problem, so instead, we drove to the centre of this small and pleasant little town and parked up outside The Old Bell pub, right next to the abbey.

This was handy, as it was the abbey we had come to see, well sort of. Malmesbury has a lot going for it, and it was previously the home of a guy called Athelstan, who came to be considered as being the first proper King of England over a thousand years ago after he displayed the strong character and leadership qualities that enabled him to unite the country for the first time ever.

But again, that is not quite why we are here. We are, in fact, here to see where Eilmer of Malmesbury lived, as he was a much more interesting character, historically speaking. While you may not have heard of him, and I hadn't before this trip, we really all should have. When you think of flight, we probably think of the Wright Brothers, or after getting this far through this book, perhaps Geoffrey de Havilland. However, a name that we should all be familiar with in this regard is, in fact, little old Eilmer.

Eilmer had been a monk here, and at some point, he had read of the Greek myth of Daedalus, who had been imprisoned on the island of Crete by King Minos. In the widely known legend, Daedalus decided to build wings of wax and feathers for himself and his son, Icarus, who was also imprisoned with him, with which they made their escape. Icarus, of course, famously flew too close to the sun, and the wax holding his feathered wings together melted, causing him to fall into the sea and drown.

Fast forward a few thousand years, and Eilmer decided to have a go at flight himself. He is said to have built a pair of wings, which is quite well documented so probably happened, and as he looked around wondering where would be the best place to attempt to fly from, he inevitably focused his attention on the top of the tower of Malmesbury

Abbey, though not the abbey we see today but a previous incarnation that was much the same height. As I looked up at the tower today, I personally figured that Eilmer must have either had a bit too much mead or was maybe a lunatic, as there is no way I would ever consider jumping off from such a height with home-made wings.

Anyway, it should probably be mentioned that although the exact date of Eilmer's flight is lost to history, it was around a thousand years ago, so just think about that for a minute. One thousand years ago, someone was attempting to fly around here. The rough date is known because it was recorded around the time of two visits of Halley's Comet in 989 and 1066, although it was obviously not known as Halley's Comet at the time.

Back to Eilmer though, and I can proudly report that, by some miracle, he somehow managed not to kill himself, but did manage to fly, or perhaps glide, for around a furlong, which is a smidge over 600 feet in English, or 200 metres for everybody else. This is quite some achievement and makes him one of the first known human beings to have ever attempted to fly, yet hardly anyone has ever heard of him.

Coming back down to earth, though, and quite literally too, Eilmer did manage to break both of his legs, so it was a bit of a hard landing. We mentioned earlier that any landing that you can walk away from is good, but with two broken legs,

I strongly suspect that Eilmer never walked anywhere ever again. His abbot forbade any further attempts at flight and literally grounded Eilmer for the rest of his life, which must have been frustrating as he was later quoted as saying that the reason he had crashed had been his lack of a tail, and he is probably right. This is amazing as it suggests at least some understanding of aerodynamics by none other than a monk around a thousand years ago. Imagine where we could be today if he had been allowed to carry on?

We walked south, passing the market cross where we sat for a moment to enjoy the view, and onto the high street, heading for Oliver's Lane, which is where some say Eilmer landed, and when we got there and looked back, it was a surprisingly long way from the abbey. It is called Oliver's Lane, but it should really be Eilmer' lane, a mistake which was down simply to a lazy scribe many moons ago, so Oliver, in fact, means Eilmer too.

Malmesbury is a lovely little town, I thought to myself, and as we wandered back up the busy high street, we decided to stop and get some food, which we sat and ate at the market cross.

The abbey beckoned us back soon enough, though, so we wandered inside to cool off as it was still really warm out, and we immediately struck up a conversation with one of the volunteer guides. I'm afraid to say I never asked her name, but she was really helpful and showed us to a stained-glass window that had recently been installed depicting Eilmer's flight. It was very pretty and colourful, depicting Eilmer in his monk's habit, but I did notice that his wings were alarmingly small. Had there been an air-accident investigation back then, I imagine they would have focused on the size of his wings as a possible cause because they really were tiny and wouldn't have helped at all.

One last thing, which I didn't have the heart to point out, though, was that they appeared to have spelt Eilmer's name wrong on the window. Oops.

Back outside, there was one last place of interest to find before we headed off to the campsite. Somewhere in the churchyard is the grave of Hannah Twynnoy, which took some finding but only because I walked right past it three times without seeing it.

There is a short poem on her gravestone that tells her story, and it turns out that poor Hanah has gone down in history for having the distinction of being the first person in England to have ever been killed by, get this, a tiger, way back in October 1703. It has to be said that tigers are not, and never have been, endemic to this country, so I just knew that there would be an interesting story here, as indeed there was.

Hannah had been working as a barmaid at a pub in the town centre at the same time as a travelling menagerie had visited the town. The show was set up behind the pub, and every time Hannah went outside, she took the trouble to taunt the animals, particularly the tiger, that were caged up out there. Unfortunately for Hannah, the quality of the cage was not what could have been called first-class back then, so when the animal ultimately escaped, it set out for a bit of revenge and chased down and killed poor Hannah Twynnoy. If there was ever anyone who regretted doing something at some point in their life, I suspect Hannah was one of them when she found herself confronted by this oversized moggy and realised that karma had truly gone full circle, for her at least.

As we made our way back to the car, we stopped to look at one last thing that our un-named guide had told us about. To the west of the main entrance, there is a wall, and this wall appears to be quite badly damaged by musket fire. She had told us that during the civil war, the town had been a Royalist Stronghold. When the Parliamentarians finally overran the town, they brought the leaders of the Royalists here and treated them to a nice firing squad, hence the damage to the wall. At least they wouldn't have had to take them far for burial, I thought to myself.

So, there you have it. Malmesbury gave us the first King of England, the first attempt at flight, and the first death by a tiger. That's a lot of firsts for Malmesbury, it has to be said.

We somehow got stuck in the rush hour leaving

the town, though luckily this only involved a little old lady on a mobility scooter blocking the road for thirty seconds, and just ten minutes later we rolled up at Southfield Farm, where we were politely told that yes, of course, we could camp there, and we could, in fact, put our tents anywhere we wanted.

The site wasn't busy, so we found a quiet corner and managed to get the tents up properly this time. It was good to clear the car out a little, as quite frankly it had become a bit messy by now, though I was still surprised when we managed to fill a carrier bag with rubbish, which went straight into the recycling bins on the site.

It was great to finally get a shower, and there was even a washing machine for us to use, which we made sure we did, and this is also when I spied a spare electrical socket and had a cunning plan. I may not have yet mentioned that there are two charging cables for the Leaf. There is the normal one, which connects the car to a dedicated charger, but there is also another one, which you can plug into any normal electrical socket of the type we all have at home, and which is often called the granny charger.

Long story short, I pulled the car up to the main building and plugged it in to top up the charge, and went back to the tent. Our clothes were still in the washing machine, so we had a cup of tea while we waited for them.

Approximately half an hour later, I went back to get the washing and found all of the sockets and lights completely dead. The car was no longer charging, and I knew immediately that I had over-loaded the circuits. I fumbled around for a fuse box and finally found it, though I did unplug the car before resetting it. I reckon it was the combination of washing machine and car on simultaneously, so I decided not to plug the car back in just yet, in case it blew it again.

Luckily, our washing was done, although it was still a bit wet. We hung it on the back of the chairs and did the only thing we could under the circum-stances – we went to the pub.

It was a thankfully short walk to the Rose and Crown in nearby Lea, and in no time at all, we were sat at the bar choosing from a fine collection of real ales. It was nice to be in clean clothes again and to have had a proper wash, of course, and we spent the next couple of hours sampling a variety of beers before finally deciding, reluctantly, I must say, that we should head back.

We had not had a lot to drink, but I certainly felt a bit giddy on the way back, and we challenged each other to see how many football chants we each knew, all of them politically incorrect and none of which are fit to print here. I am proud, or perhaps ashamed to say that we knew rather a lot, but I put this down to the fact that we had both worked in a football stadium at one time or another. I was about to start another when I heard a splash and realised that I had fallen into a stream.

THAMES HEAD

I awoke in the morning and wondered why my socks were damp, and then realised that all of me was damp. I sat up and looked around and immediately realised that I was not in my tent, which was something of a surprise, but I was on the floor next to a washing machine.

Hearing snoring from above me, I discovered that Robin was asleep on a kitchen worktop, which was yet another surprise, and as I stood up, I saw that he too was rather wet, or at least his trousers were. I wondered for a moment whether or not he had had an accident in the night but then had a flashback of falling into a raging torrent and Robin rushing in to save me from drowning. I couldn't find my phone, which could be a problem as my bank card was with it, and the only positive thing I can take from waking up was that someone had remembered to plug the car back in, and it was now fully charged.

Rob stirred into life, and after he had a good stretch and nearly fell off the worktop, we went on a hunt for my phone. Tracing our steps from the previous night, we came upon the raging torrent that had almost taken my life, only to find out that it was, in fact, a small stream barely a few inches deep. For some undefined reason, I then remembered ringing my wife late last night and professing my love for her, and I remember that I did this while sat on a washing machine, obviously, so we headed back to the campsite.

We both searched high and low and even looked in the washing machine, immediately after which Robin found my phone. Again, this is when it came back to me that I had cleverly thought to put my phone somewhere safe, which is presumably when I put it in the fridge. All I can say is that the Rose and Crown do great beer, and it's as simple as that.

After another shower, this time not for hygiene reasons, I finally felt almost human again and discovered that Robin, in a further demonstration of his greatness, had somehow managed to cook us up a sausage and egg sandwich. I did wonder momentarily how long the sausages had been in the car, but only for a second or so as I also remembered that they had been in a cool box.

The double helping of coffee further helped to bring me back to life, and as I became more aware of my surroundings, I realised that everyone else on the campsite was still asleep and that it was still, in fact, not even six o'clock.

By seven, we had managed to wash and pack everything away and were ready to go, but I decided that Rob would have to drive as I suspected I had drunk a little bit more than him last night, so I had better be careful. I figured, however, that I had not even had four pints, as we had been on halves so we could sample the many strange and fantastical ales on offer, and wondered if it had been the mix of drinks that had left me somewhat worse for wear, but decided instead that I simply cannot take my beer, and is why I rarely drink the stuff.

We had a third coffee, which also gave us a chance to plan a route for the day, and by the time we were getting ready to leave, the other campers had finally started to drift out of their tents, and some of them looked familiar from the night before. By the looks of them, several had also thought it a good idea to have a wander down to the Rose and Crown, though none of them looked like they had fallen into a river on the way back.

After discussing our progress so far, Rob and I decided that we would have to really pull our fingers out and get a move on, and stop enjoying ourselves so much. It was a long way to the Scottish border from where we were, and our progress over the last two days had been what can only be described as dismal, as well, of course, as still glacial.

Not all of the problem, though, was down to us enjoying ourselves. We were spending so much time in places simply because we were waiting for the car to charge, so we decided to redouble our efforts to find rapid chargers wherever we could. We also decided that we might have to miss out on a few of the places we had planned to visit, which would be tough, as so many of them were not only places that we had never been to before but were also places that looked incredibly interesting.

We decided, though, that the first two places on our list for today were too important to miss, with the first one being the little town of Tetbury, and the second one being the source of the mighty Thames, so bidding farewell to our fellow but still sleepy campers, we drove down the bumpy track that led us back to the road, and headed north to Tetbury.

There was only one charger in town at the Close Hotel, though it proved to be out of order. We had a quick walk around the town, which was not as nice as Malmesbury as far as I was concerned, although I imagined not many places could be.

It cannot be all that bad, though, as Highgrove lies just to the southwest of the town, home to Prince Charles, future king of England. I often wonder how long the queen will go on for and hope it is a long time indeed; otherwise, I shall have to re-edit this book, which would be a pain.

As we walked around the town, we kept seeing dolphins, which appeared to be some kind of mascot for the place, and I found this odd because we were so many miles from the sea. For instance, there are nineteen of the things hanging from just the Market House alone.

It turns out that there is a far-fetched tale of a dolphin saving a ship variously going to either Ireland or America, carrying either famous people or the whole of the town's wealth, but it all sounds a bit fishy to me.

Tetbury is just to the west of the watershed, so we had to head east a short while to get to the source of the River Thames, also known as Thames Head. When I looked at the map, it truly surprised me that the source of this most famous river is so far over here in the west of England, just a short distance from the River Severn that takes water in completely the opposite direction towards the Atlantic. In fact, the straight-line distance to the Bristol Channel is only around 30 miles as the crow flies or the pigeon for that matter, but an astonishing 120 miles to the North Sea in the other direction.

As you would expect, we parked up in a pub, in this case, the Thames Head public house, which was very nice but did not have a public charger. Again, this was not so much of a problem, but as we were going to be leaving the car here for quite a while so we could walk to the actual source of the river, I thought I would be cheeky.

I went inside and spoke to a young man behind the bar and explained what we were doing and why. He, in turn, went off to find a supervisor, and when he returned with a young lady who looked about as old as my youngest child, which would be to say eleven, I explained myself all over again. I had basically asked if we could plug the car in, perhaps through one of the windows, and when she declined my offer, my first reaction was never mind, we could charge later in Cirencester, just down the road. But then she immediately followed up by explaining to me that the pub had a small campsite around the back and that I could drive around there where I would find an outside socket available for use, and as a bonus, it was free of charge.

I thanked her profusely, moved the car around to the camp ground, and with that, Rob and I were off on our hunt to track down the source of the River Thames.

This turned out to be very easy, in fact embarrassingly easy, as the path was not only well laid out but incredibly well signposted. After just ten minutes of walking, we were at the stone marker that signifies the river's source but were disappointed to find that it was dry today, and there was not a drop of water in sight. This is not surprising, given the heat of the last few days, or even weeks, and in fact, the source of the Thames is not in one place as such, as how could it be, but could be one of many springs around this area. The spring we were at now, which was of course not a spring at all at the moment, was located in a small meadow called Trewsbury Mead and was simply the highest of all the springs around here. Another school of thought says this place is not the source of the Thames at all, though, and apparently, some river spotters get a bit upset at this, but more of that later.

Anyway, from here, the river slowly meanders eastwards, joined by many other tributaries along the way, gradually increasing in size as it goes. Passing through seven counties as it goes along and going through delights such as Oxford and Windsor, and of course London, the Thames has played a huge role in the country's history. Surprisingly, there are more than 80 islands in the Thames, and the river is crossed by over 200 bridges between here and the sea.

Perhaps most surprisingly, though, is the fact that the river has, for many centuries, been possibly the favourite place for murderers to dispose of their victims. This includes the somewhat unknown Amelia Dyer, who may, in fact, be the most prolific serial killer the country has ever seen, and maybe even the world. Dyer lived in Victorian times, which was, of course, an era of great poverty for some, if not most people. Dyer saw an opportunity to earn money by becoming a baby farmer, which is exactly what it sounds like. Poor people would pay her small amounts of money to look after their babies.

However, many baby farmers did not take great care of the children, and many would die of neglect. Dyer, however, took this to a whole new level and systematically murdered dozens and probably hundreds of babies by strangling them no sooner than their mothers had dropped them off and then gone away to do whatever it was they had to do. Some estimates put the total at 400, which would make her history's most prolific killer.

She would dispose of the bodies in the Thames and was only discovered when the tiny corpse of one baby was discovered in a bag in the river, with evidence pointing directly to her. Tried and convicted in true Victorian efficiency, Dyer became known as the Ogress of Reading, and rather fittingly perhaps, she was finally hanged in Newgate Prison in 1896. As she was alive at the time of the Jack the Ripper murders, some even speculated that Dyer could, in fact, have been the ripper, but there is no real evidence for this, so it remains just wild speculation.

The river must have been positively full of bodies bobbing merrily along during Victorian times, and we could talk all day about such things, but I am going to mention just one more, as I feel it is really worth it. At around the same time as Amelia Dyer was up to her dastardly deeds, another murder occurred that was even more horrific and was at least as bad as the murder of sweet Fanny Adams, possibly more so, leading me to wonder what was wrong with everybody back then.

The case in question is that of the murder of Julia

Thomas in March 1879, who was chopped up, boiled, and offered as food to the manager of a local pub, The Hole in the Wall, as well as to the local street children, in the form of lard and dripping. Not surprisingly, she didn't prove popular as a snack, so the murderer, none other than Julia's maid, who went by the name of Kate Webster, simply dumped most of the body parts into the Thames, where much of it was found though not the head, it should be noted. Sentenced to death by hanging, Webster tried in vain to avoid the death penalty by then claiming to be pregnant, but this was dismissed, and she was hanged in July of that same year, once again thanks to ruthless Victorian efficiency. Webster finally confessed to her crime the night before her hanging but still never gave up the location of Julia Thomas' missing melon.

Fast forward a hundred years or so, and a chap you have probably heard of, Sir David Attenborough, him of fishes and all things nature, decided to do some renovations at The Hole in the Wall pub in 2010. He had bought the dilapidated building to redevelop it, as he was presumably sick of the sight of the place, which had been slowly crumbling away next to his own house. While digging foundations out at the rear of the pub, then, Attenborough and his builders were presumably somewhat surprised when they found a human skull, and suspicions arose immediately that it was the one that had belonged to Julia Thomas, because let's face it, there cannot be that many human body parts buried randomly around us, surely?

Unfortunately, nobody knew where the rest of Thomas had been buried, so DNA testing was not possible. However, carbon-dating certainly placed the remains in the correct era, and other testing revealed that the remains had low collagen levels, which is consistent with boiling, apparently. The coroner, then, was more than satisfied and subsequently declared that the skull was indeed that of Julia Thomas, and she was finally laid to rest in Richmond Cemetery, once again close to the River Thames.

Getting back to the task at hand, however, and I have to say that there is not a lot for us to see at the source of a river that turns out to be dry, so within minutes we were on our way back to the pub to enjoy a nice cold coke. We were lucky that the pub had been open for breakfasts, as we also needed to use their bathroom facilities, and after all was done and dusted, we went to get the car, which was once again more or less fully charged.

We drove back the way we came and headed for Sapperton, where I wanted to visit another grave. Please don't think that is a dark or gory thing to do; it is just interesting. This one, in particular, is that of Sir Stafford Cripps, who may not be that well known but had an interesting life. He held many positions in government both before, during and after the war and was at one time being considered to replace Winston Churchill himself. I remember a funny story from my university days that is worth repeating, and involves both Cripps and Churchill and starts when Cripps attended Churchill's chambers in the Houses of Parliament at the height of the Second World War. Churchill was on the toilet at the time, and when his butler informed him that Cripps wanted to see him, Churchill told him to tell Cripps he *could only deal with one shit at a time.*

The grave looked forgotten and neglected, standing under a tree at the edge of the graveyard, and it felt quite sad to be there, so we did not hang about. We would have gone in the church, but it was locked, so instead, we moved on. As we left the village, we noticed that there is a small river just to the north of the village, the River Frome, which we did not need to cross, and although the Thames took everything east, the Frome took everything west, so we were still very much on the watershed. The Frome rises near Brimpsfield, our next destination, a few miles to our north and thus marks another point on the watershed, though this is not the only reason we are going there, as I wanted to see if the village looked familiar to me. The place, you see, was once the setting for a BBC television series that I enjoyed greatly when it was on, and which was considered by many to be science fiction at the time, though now I am not so sure. You will understand when we get there.

We parked in the centre of the village and made our way towards the church, but I did not recognise a single thing, which left me somewhat disappointed. Brimpsfield had actually been the fictional location for *Survivors*, a 1970s BBC TV series that saw Peter and Abbey Grant struggling to cope in the aftermath of a pandemic inadvertently released by a Chinese scientist, I kid you not. How art imitates life? Or is it the other way around? I'm just not sure anymore. Anyway, I had never actually seen the 1970s version.

I am, however, familiar with the 2008 remake of the series, which was in part brought about by the recent SARS outbreak, which caused BBC producers some concern about both that and any future pandemics, and this was perhaps their way of getting the word out. Ironically, the second season was postponed by the real-life Swine Flu pandemic in 2009, which of course, was just a taste of things to come for us all. Rob and I decided that, upon reflection, we didn't want to hang around in Brimpsfield after all.

The village's only other claim to fame was that it once had a rather impressive castle, so we went off to find it somewhere near to the church. There wasn't a lot to see, other than a plaque and a mound of earth, which seemed to have been used as somewhere to bury dead people at some point. The plaque told us that we were in the right place and that this had once been the home of the Giffard family until 1322. This date is very specific, as indeed it can be because this is the year when the last lord of the manor, John Giffard, managed to annoy the king, at the time Edward II, so much that he had Giffard executed and then went one step further and had his castle completely destroyed as well. I'm not sure what Giffard did, but he certainly knew how to push the king's buttons, that's for sure.

Coberley is just a few minutes' drive away, but it feels longer as we navigate a series of tiny roads to get there. The village feels a bit tight, so we park near the church, always a good option, and look at the map to find out exactly where we want to be. We are, in fact, looking for a place called Seven Springs, which is supposed to be very close to this village, though it turns out that it is actually quite a walk and we could have driven a lot closer. After a democratic vote, we made a unanimous decision to drive another mile or so, which will save us a good hour overall, when you take into account the time spent staring at a (hopefully) wet hole in the ground as well as the time spent on the walk back.

It turns out that the Seven Springs we end up at is, in fact, a pub and is one of those large chain ones that welcome, of all things, children. They are everywhere, and the management has even had the audacity to build a playground for the little devils, which will surely only attract more of them. To top it off, at the time of our visit, children everywhere were enjoying weeks of summer downtime, which means the place is doubly busy, despite the relatively early hour, but we are here now, and really need to visit this place, so off we go.

We venture through the pub, resisting the temptation for a nice cold Coke, and disappear out the back, which is where the fabled seven springs are supposed to be. Hopping over a fence, and I am not sure we really should have, so please don't try this, we do indeed find what seems to be the source of the River Churn, although I found it difficult to get to seven when I tried counting the springs.

When I mentioned the controversy earlier about the true source of the River Thames, this exact spot at Seven Springs is one of the contenders. The River Churn flows south almost all the way across the beautiful Cotswolds and joins the River Thames at Cricklade after passing through Cirencester. If the Churn were to be counted as a tributary of the Thames, as it clearly should be because there is no argument that says it does not flow into the Thames, that this would make Seven Springs further from the mouth of the Thames than actual Thames Head itself, and by a not inconsiderable 14-miles. I probably do not need to remind you that we have also just been to Thames Head. It was, well, dry, so how that place can be considered the river's true source is beyond me. Apparently, I am not alone, and this is because it is potentially very important, you see. Do even a basic amount of research into the longest rivers in England, and you will instantly find that the River Severn at 220-miles, just to our west, is slightly longer than the Thames, which is allegedly 215 miles. Simple maths tells us that if you add the missing 14-miles of the Churn onto the Thames, then it becomes 9-miles longer than the Severn, so maybe the Thames really is the longest river in England after all. Perhaps the nice people at Ordnance Survey could sort this out?

Fighting our way through crowds of ravenous children, we make it back to the car somehow alive and consider our next steps. Gloucester is just down the road, with a Tesco and its promise of chargers, so we head there just to restock on drinks, really. The supermarket is on the outskirts of town, and while we let the car charge, which should not take long, we once again venture around the fridges and freezers to cool off, as the day has once again grown uncomfortably hot. I did notice a security guard following us at one point, so I instructed Rob to act shifty, and I did the same. However, he must have realised we were messing around, as, after a few minutes, he left us alone.

I also considered a game of supermarket bingo but decided against it on the grounds that I was a grown man and not a 6-year-old boy. Supermarket Bingo, you see, is where you venture around the shop, placing as many items as you can into other people's trolleys, and then follow them through the checkout. I have done this many times with my apprentices, also known as my children, and it is quite amusing when the person actually buys whatever you have added to their trolley, despite presumably knowing full well that they did not put whatever it was in there. In my many years of doing this, I have helped people buy all sorts of rubbish that they never knew they wanted, such as barbecue tongs, five-kilogram bags of rice, and my personal favourite, a deluxe frozen lobster. The lady who bought the lobster stands out the most in my memory. She was even using one of those self-service tills, which I will not use, by the way, and I watched her pick it up, stare at it for ten seconds, and then scan it anyway. Priceless.

We paid for our drinks and went back out to the car, and when I looked at my notes, I realised we were in Brockworth. The supermarket stood on the site of an old airfield and has links to another first in the world of aviation, for this very spot was the site of the first-ever flight of a jet-powered aircraft in Britain, built by none other than Frank Whittle. We even beat the Americans at this, which is always good, although the Germans and Italians had already managed a handful of flights. The aeroplane, in particular, was the Gloster E28/39, which is an odd name or is perhaps the result of someone not being able to spell Gloucester. It only managed to fly to a height of about five feet, and although there is no sign of what went on here anymore, there is a life-sized model of the aircraft on a roundabout somewhere in the midlands which I had seen many years ago, but could not quite remember exactly where.

We are also very close to Coopers Hill, which is more or less just across the road, and you have probably heard of this at some point. Every year, or at least every year when the world has not been in the grip of a pandemic, lunatics from around the world gather together here to chase a large piece of cheese down a very steep hill. Fortunately for us, the health and safety police have not yet managed to shut this down, which is the right decision as I believe it is the right of any individual to be as stupid as they want to be. Indeed, I accomplish this every day, and it is the only thing I am good at, to be honest.

One last little thing to say about Gloucester while we rub shoulders with it is that the Queen Mother used to stop at the same newsagents in the town every time she went to the races in nearby Cheltenham, which was pretty often, I imagine. I am told by a reliable source that her order was always the same, being a packet of ciggies and a bottle of gin.

The next twenty or so miles were a blast, and we made good progress indeed. We bypassed Cheltenham, home of course to the secret services of this country and their large doughnut-shaped building, and passed through Prestbury, which is supposedly the most haunted village in Britain and is perhaps why we chose not to stop there. We then drove to and considered climbing up Cleeve Hill, which at 1,083 feet is the highest point in the beautiful Cotswolds, but decided that it would be silly in the heat of the day and continued on to Belas Knapp, where we most certainly made sure we got out of the car.

Belas Knapp is possibly the finest example of a stone-age burial chamber around. Dozens of bodies were found in it when it was excavated, and I am happy to report that it has been fully restored to its original glory. We are talking full-on Indiana Jones stuff here, with false entrances on either side and chambers to explore. Most importantly, the barrow is free to enter.

From the barrow, we drove the short route into Winchcombe and sat outside of a small semi-detached house for a while on a street called The Hyde. It didn't look like anyone was in, but I ventured over and knocked on the door anyway, though nobody answered.

It would have been nice if someone had answered, as this was the house where a meteorite fell to earth in February 2021, putting the small town well and truly on the map. The Wilcock family had briefly become local celebrities and had certainly spoken to the BBC among others, as this had marked the first time a meteorite had landed in the UK since 1991, when one had crashed down at Glatton, near Peterborough. The Winchcombe one was said to be very special, and while there are over 65,000 meteorites in collections around the world, there are only about fifty of the type that fell on Winchcombe.

Incidentally, NASA has recently spent tens of millions of dollars on missions to send out probes to get exactly the same kind of material that landed on a suburban driveway in a small market town, while we managed to just pick one up in the suburbs, which I am sure you will agree, surely leaves a good taste in the mouth, right?

This reminds me of a story from the height of the space race, which tells of NASA's mission to put millions of dollars into a project to develop a pen that works in zero gravity, as traditional ball-point pens rely specifically on gravity and don't work up there. The Russians, on the other hand, simply used a pencil.

Unfortunately, like all good urban legends, there is not much truth to this. The space pen, as it became known, was actually developed by a guy called Paul Fisher, and although it did indeed cost him a lot of money to develop it, he made money from it in the end, selling it to both NASA and the Russians alike, as well as anyone else who wanted to buy one. Still, it is a good story.

Before someone reported us as peeping-toms or accused us of casing out a house for a possible burglary, we were off again, this time to the delightful village of Snowshill. We parked the car discreetly out of the way, so we didn't spoil the beautiful views, as it was a photograph of the place that we were after. I asked Robin if he thought the place looked familiar, and he said it did though he did not know why, and when I told him where he had seen it before, he realised immediately.

This village actually featured as one of the filming locations for the blockbuster movie *Bridget Jones's Diary*. At the beginning of the film, Jones is seen arriving in a taxi at her parents' house in the village in an incredibly snowy scene, which makes the name of the place even more appropriate. We stood near the church at the top of a hill and re-created the scene as best as we could, but we didn't have a taxi.

We wanted to be in Chipping Campden to get some lunch, so we decided to make just one more stop, and that would be at the Broadway Tower. We had plenty of miles on the car to get us to both places, and there would be a choice of chargers there when we arrived, so we took a leisurely drive via the backroads to the tower, which lay just a couple of miles outside of the town.

We parked at the café at the bottom of the hill and decided to reward ourselves with a drink upon our return, where we could also rest after our walk. It's not that it was a long walk, but again it was ridiculously hot, and quite frankly, too hot for walking.

The tower was worth it anyway, and I reckoned it would make a fine house. The history is interesting, too, and it was built for a member of the upper classes called Lady Coventry. She clearly had more money than sense, as the reason she had it built was to see if she could see it from her house in Worcester, which was 22-miles away. The tower is very well-known around here now, but what is not perhaps quite as well-known is the fact that there is now a nuclear bunker underneath it, which was put there in the 1950s, just in case. If you snoop around, you will see the hatch.

The place was pretty busy today, so once again, we didn't hang about and were soon sat in the café enjoying a civilised cappuccino and a slice of cake. We sat outside the back of the café and managed to grab ourselves a table with a parasol, which helped us to stay at least a little cooler. Hopefully, this would be the hottest part of the day, and things would soon start cooling down, as although we had both had showers recently, we agreed that we felt as if we had not had one for at least a month. Thank goodness we had our own tents, I thought to myself.

While we were enjoying our calories, I looked at the app that showed us where the chargers were and realised I had made a big mistake. I am not sure what town I had been looking at, but it turns out that Chipping Campden only had one charging option, but that was a Tesla destination, which is to say that it is really for charging Tesla cars only. There is sometimes the ability to use one of the chargers on other, lesser, electric cars, but this is far from guaranteed, so after much discussion, we decided to head elsewhere rather than risk arriving somewhere and having to call out the breakdown people again and end up in a hole in the woods.

To be fair, we were in no rush to charge and reckoned we could easily make it to Banbury, even after taking into account the handful of stops we wished to make in the meantime. As a double bonus, I had never been to Banbury, other than our brief stop for a charge on the way down here, so that would be a treat in itself.

Our first stop was the grammatically displeasing Moreton-in-Marsh, and I found myself wanting to add 'the' in there somewhere. I say stop, but we never actually stopped but simply drove past a pub called the Prancing Pony. If you go there yourself, I should perhaps tell you that the real name of the pub is The Bell Inn, and was, in fact, the local pub of none other than John Tolkien, or J.R.R. Tolkien, who of course wrote The Lord of the Rings, though I'm sure you knew that. What you perhaps did not know is that he based the Prancing Pony, the pub in the story, on the Bell Inn. If you ever look at pictures of the two, you might be able to see where the influence came from because Rob and I both agreed that we certainly could, even from the outside.

The next stop was, in fact, a stop and was just a mile or two down the road. In retrospect, I might not have stopped if I had to live through the experience again knowing what I know now, as the left turn came upon us rather quickly and resulted in the 40-ton lorry that was more or less stuck to my bumper having to make creative use of both his horn, which was very effective and his brakes, which were not so.

Anyway, we lived to see another day and jumped out of the car to admire the Four Shire Stone. Sounding like something else out of one of Tolkien's stories, it is clear that he was influenced by places in this area, and quite probably this stone.

Historically, it marked the boundaries of Warwickshire, Oxfordshire, Gloucestershire and Worcestershire, though due to some tinkering in the 1930s, Worcestershire no longer extends this far east. Nonetheless, Robin and I took turns jumping across the road, visiting three counties in as many seconds, until the driver of a lorry carrying a skip nearly ran us down.

We had not had to venture off our route for this stop and were doing well with the miles, so we decided to next head for the Rollright Stones, which we had originally intended to bypass. On the way there, though, we had an unscheduled stop at Barton on the Heath, as we realised that we had forgotten about this little place. It had been the home of a man called Robert Dover, and he had revived the Olympics sometime in the 1600s, though he called them The Cotswold Games, or alternatively the Olimpicks. They ran on and off until the mid-1800s, and I only mention this because as Rob and I are doing this journey, the Olympics as we know it is underway halfway across the world in Japan. We did have a quick poke around in the church but sadly found no reference to either Robert or his Olimpicks. There has been an attempt to revive Dover's Olimpicks recently, though, and perhaps a highlight of this is the shin-kicking competition which is now held at nearby Dover's Hill. Opponents line up at sunset and, facing each other in some kind of macho stare off, grab each other's shoulders and then attempt to kick their opponents in the shins, which I can vouch is very painful. I was going to suggest to Robin that we have a go at this, but as he is a lot bigger than me, I decided to keep my mouth firmly shut.

We pulled into a layby that had been conveniently built immediately adjacent to the Rollright Stones, and for which we were very grateful as it meant we did not have to walk far in today's heat. Although the day was getting on, it had not cooled down, and if anything, I would say it was even hotter than before.

We crossed the road to first have a look at the King Stone, an oddly shaped monolith standing all alone in the middle of a field. It is variously thought to be a marker or something to do with astronomy, though nobody really knows, but in my opinion, this only adds to the air of mystery. This whole area, of course, is famous for standing stones, which begs the question, why here?

We found the stone circle back across the road, and although I did not realise it at the time, we had crossed over from Warwickshire, where the King Stone stands, and into Oxfordshire, where the rest of the stones live.

As we stood within the stone circle, I would like to say I felt some mysterious energy or something, but I cannot, although I can honestly say it was still very hot. Although the circle is obviously ancient, judging by the apparent erosion of the stones, it still offered a feeling of completeness, and the name given to the stones, which is the King's Men, somehow seems appropriate. Rob and I discussed how on earth someone had managed to move them in position, and while he talked of pulleys and hoists, I told Rob that he was wrong and that the aliens did it. For a minute, I thought he took me seriously until his eyes rolled and he realised he was wasting his time.

The highlight of the day was coming up at Hook Norton, and I tried to big it up a bit to Rob but refused to tell him where we were going, or more accurately, what we were going to see. On the way there in the car, I gave him a clue that it was red and told him that if he guessed what we would find in the church, I would buy him a crate of beer.

He had a go and guessed first that we would find the holy grail, which was clearly silly because that was never red, and his second guess was a crying statue or some other miracle related item that was maybe bleeding. While that was not necessarily a bad guess, he was still way out, though he refused to use his third guess until he had thought about it. I watched him like a hawk to make sure he didn't use his phone to cheat, as I wouldn't trust him as far as I could throw him, which is not very far, to be honest, being the big unit that he is.

We parked up and approached the church, and as we did so, I gave Rob one last chance to guess what was inside, but he went for the world's largest organ, thereby missing out on a crate of beer. I opened the door, which was thankfully unlocked, and I must say I would have been gutted if it had been locked. As our eyes adjusted to the dimly lit interior, there it was, directly in front of us in all its glory, and the it, in particular, was the village's fire engine, shining bright red against the neutral colours of the church, and looking as great as it probably did when it was built.

Robin thought it odd to find a fire engine in a church, but this apparently unusual find was once quite common, and in fact, made a lot of sense. Way back in the 1600s, the authorities that ran Oxford ordered all parishes to buy and maintain a fire engine. At the time, the decision to store them in churches made perfect sense. If you think about it, everyone knew where the church was; they were usually kept unlocked, and churches were generally in the middle of the village. The one before us is perhaps the only surviving one left in a church and has therefore been given a name and is known as the *Sentinel*, which is quite fitting, I reckon, and was reported as being in use right up until the 1890s. And if you're wondering why Oxford, in particular, would compel the purchase of fire engines by all parishes, just bear in mind how many thatched cottages there are today, and imagine how many there were in centuries gone by.

With nothing else to see here, we headed off to Banbury, which would be our last stop today, we decided. There were still many miles left on the old Leaf, and we got to the town without any problems and soon enough found the charger at the local Tesco. Wandering down the hill into the town itself, our thoughts turned to food and somewhere to stay, with both problems being addressed in the exact same order. While Rob went into a takeaway to get us both curry and chips, I looked for somewhere to camp and found a campsite just up the road at the Old Forge. A quick phone call confirmed that they had room for us, and after a quick wander down to have a look at the cross, as in Banbury Cross, we were walking back to the car with our new best mate, Karl, who was cycling around the south of England just for something to do. He had stopped to ask us if there was anything interesting to see in the town, and other than the cross which he had just cycled past, we apologised and said that we were not aware of anything else, no offence Banbury. When he asked us which cross we were talking about, we pointed straight at it, just over his shoulder, and wondered how on earth he had missed it. He left us to go and have a look at a large church and presumably the cross, and we walked back to the car, drove to the campsite, showered and went straight to bed. We were shattered.

HANGED, DRAWN
AND QUARTERED

We woke up, once again, before any other campers, at the ridiculously early hour of 4.30am. Of course, we were doing this intentionally, as it gave us more hours of daylight with which we could explore England, but I mentioned to Rob that I was a bit of a wimp and figured I could not go on with so little sleep for much longer.

Thankfully, he fully agreed and went one step further by suggesting we try to speed up our progress if this was somehow possible. After a couple of minutes spent talking about this, we figured we only had a couple of ways that we could do this, which basically meant using only rapid chargers while at the same time not making as many stops. While both things were theoretically possible, we didn't want to spoil our trip, so instead decided just to try and plan our days a bit better. We had previously just been driving around the country with a paper map, deciding where to head next and then seeing where the chargers were, so we wondered if this process would be more efficient if given a little planning beforehand and figured we had nothing to lose.

With that in mind, and with everything packed away, our first destination was Hellidon, just a few miles to the north-east, and which would see us cross the route of HS2, the new high-speed rail line that is being built from London to the north, which will help commuters heading down to the big-smoke get an extra half-hour in bed, bless them, all at the bargain price to the taxpayer of a mere hundred billion pounds.

I thought we might see some sign of the work, but alas, we did not, so a few minutes later, we pulled up at Hellidon, where you will find Hellidon Test Track, also known as Catesby Tunnel. Unfortunately, the nearest we could get was a view from a bridge, which was not a view of much really, which was a shame.

Hellidon is right on the watershed, which is split here by a line generally running northeast, but it is the tunnel that is of interest, to be honest. An old Victorian railway tunnel, which was only built because the lord of the manor, Henry Attenborough, objected to seeing unsightly steam trains passing through his land, has now been converted into a state-of-the-art test track for cars. At over a mile and a half long, people such as the Stig can hurl down the road that has been built in there at a hundred miles per hour, all without a speed camera in sight. We really couldn't see a way to get any closer, so we headed back to the car and continued north, although considerably slower than a hundred miles per hour.

Once again, I began to think about what is the north of England and the south, as we figured we had just crossed into Northampton. Don't let the north part of the name fool you, though, as I reckoned we were still very much in the south, but don't worry, I'll let you know when we really are in the north.

We passed through Staverton without stopping, as there was nothing there to make us stop, although a long-distance footpath passed through the village. The Jurassic Way runs from Banbury to Stamford, and I suggested to Rob that we put it on our to-do list, which he agreed with, and I wondered what dinosauric delights awaited walkers on that path.

Several roundabouts greeted us as we followed the ring-road around Daventry, and they were seemingly all of the normal variety, did not appear to have been designed by someone high on crack cocaine, and did not require a degree in quantum mechanics to navigate. Although we were not stopping here, however, primarily due to the early hour and the fact that the town was therefore shut, it was here that some boffins first tested radar in 1935, and thank goodness they did, otherwise we might now all be speaking German. I have nothing against Germans or their language;

indeed, I do actually speak *ein bisschen*, but I prefer my own mother tongue, thank you very much. Basically, without the advantage of radar in the Second World War, we would have lost the Battle of Britain, heavily outnumbered as our pilots were. And in order not to make the enemy suspicious about how we were managing to shoot down so many of their aircraft, the air ministry created a cunning ruse about carrots, which is why we still say to this day that eating carrots improves your eyesight, which is basically a load of old tosh. While we are on this subject, when someone tells you that reading in the dark will damage your eyesight, that's a load of old tosh, too.

Before we leave the town, it is also worth mentioning the tale of James Hawker, who also came from Daventry. You've probably never heard of him, but he went down in history as the most successful poacher ever to come out of England, and he was a bit of a lad. He joined the local militia, as there wasn't an army as such back then, just so he could get a gun, and then infiltrated the ranks of the landed gentry by somehow managing to get himself elected to the local school board, where he could befriend the very men that he intended to rob, therefore gaining a considerable advantage. He kept up the ruse almost his entire life, with some only figuring out what had happened when Hawker finally died in 1921. He is buried a few miles away in Leicester, and it is his gravestone that gives the game away, as it is amusingly engraved with the line, *I will poach til I die*. He even wrote a book about his exploits, so brazen was he. I liked this guy, I decided.

Within a couple of minutes, we were at Ashby-St-Ledgers, and we were going to have a quick stop here so we could have a look at a place that is insignificant in itself but is a huge part of our history. At the east end of the main street, which funnily enough is called Main Street, and next to the church, stands all that remains of the manor house that once belonged to Robert Catesby. You may know him from school history lessons, as he was one of the main conspirators involved in the Gunpowder Plot, and it is in fact here, in the room above the gatehouse, that much of that plot was, well, plotted. It appears to be someone's house nowadays, so it appears that a look is all we will get today.

We continued north and only had a couple of more miles left on the road we were on, which had, in fact, turned out to be the longest three-digit road in the country, the A361, and which ended at the next village, which was Kilsby. Unfortunately, this was the village's only claim to fame, and seeming as it was a bit of a rubbish one, we headed next to Naseby, the site of the famous battlefield of the same name and slap-bang on the watershed.

We parked up in the village on a road called Newlands and got out to stretch our legs. There were a couple of dog walkers out and about, despite the early hour, and we got talking to one of them, and her name was Miriam. She commented on how scruffy our car was, though she was quite diplomatic and asked us if we were camping what with all the tents and stuff in the back window, and I was almost tempted to tell her no we were not, and ask her whatever gave her that impression. I can be a bit of an idiot like that sometimes, but I was only almost tempted, like I said.

We told her that we were attempting to drive up the country in between all of the rivers and to follow the watershed, and she raised her eyebrows and told us that we had hit the jackpot by coming to Ashby-St-Ledgers. Rob and I looked at each other, not knowing what she meant, but then she went on to tell us that in the garden behind us, literally next to where we had parked, there was a cone that marked the source of the River Avon, which flows west from here, ultimately dumping millions of gallons into the River Severn, and then, of course, the Atlantic.

In no time at all, she had opened the gate to the farm, despite our protestations, and she insisted that no, the owner would not mind at all and was used to people trampling their rhododendrons and marigolds. Unfortunately, a large holly bush guarded the cone, which bit me as I moved in for a better look. There before us, though, was what looked like a Victorian traffic cone and written upon it was *Source of the Avon 1822*. I presume the date signified the cone being placed there and not when the river first popped up.

Rob had also been mauled by the holly bush, as he had found it even harder than me to duck beneath it, given that he was about eleven feet tall, and a small trickle of blood ran right down the middle of his forehead. I considered telling him, as quite frankly it looked a bit strange, but decided on reflection that this would not be fair, as it would deprive people of something funny to look at for the next few hours.

There are other rivers around here that spring up and flow in completely different directions, specifically the River Ise, which ultimately ends up discharging into The Wash and then the North Sea, and also the River Welland a mile or two away, which goes in the same direction, so we really were right in the middle of the watershed at this point.

We thanked Miriam, who wandered on her way, waving goodbye once or twice and hauling her clearly elderly dog along. Robin commented that this had been an unexpected bonus, as indeed it had been, and with that, we were off again. We drove north, intending to find Naseby Field, site of the famous battle, and soon enough came across a sign that pointed to a monument, suggesting we were in the right place. There was a handy layby, which was empty, so we dumped the car and headed across the field towards the memorial in the distance.

There was a small path of sorts at the edge of the field, and as the rest of it had been ploughed, this was very handy. We were soon at the memorial, called the Cromwell Memorial, and enjoyed views all around of where the battle presumably took place. I am not sure what we expected, but all we could see were fields, which kind of makes sense, but the memorial was certainly a bonus. An engraving told us that Oliver Cromwell led the cavalry charge on June 14th 1645, which decided the outcome of the battle and the fate of the war, as this result made a Royalist victory impossible. The king hung on, though, as kings tend to do, and Charles did not surrender until almost a year later. This is possibly because he knew what fate awaited him, and he was finally executed on 30 January 1649, after being put on trial and found guilty of treason, the first time this had happened to a king.

Funnily enough, the man charged with prosecuting Charles I came from a village just up the road, and that would be Husbands Bosworth. By some strange twist of fate, the village is also exactly on the watershed that divides England up at this point, so it is there that we head next. We nearly never made it, as rounding a bend, a truck coming the other way decided to use all of the road, the driver presumably thinking that there would be no possibility whatsoever that another vehicle would be on the roads today. Well, our brakes worked, and his did too, although his load, which consisted of half a dozen shiny new cars, nearly tipped over, an occurrence that would have seen us ending up like something resembling a pancake.

Near-death experience happily avoided, we pulled up outside the Bell End pub, oh I am so sorry, I mean the Bell Inn. I was still thinking of that crazy truck driver, clearly. The village was, unfortunately, not very exciting, especially at this time of the morning. It was beginning to come alive, although how alive exactly that would be, it was hard to say, as there just seemed to be nothing here. We walked down to the church, which was nice but locked, and sat for a while at the base of an old market cross, watching the traffic go by and breathing in lots of nice lovely fumes. I said to Rob that if we did this trip in a few years, then there might be more electric cars and thus less fumes at least, though I reckoned that Husbands Bosworth would still have an odd name and would still be, well, boring.

Anyway, its claim to fame is that the man who prosecuted Charles I came from here, as I said earlier. John Cook was baptised at the church just behind us, All Saints, in 1608. However, the family farm was a few miles away at Burbage. He went on to go down in history as the first lawyer to successfully prosecute a head of state in a trial that began on 20 January 1649, changing history forever. By 26 January, the trial was over, the King had been found guilty of high treason, and he had, of course, lost his head. Unfortunately, however, Cook ultimately backed the wrong side. With the Restoration of the Monarchy in 1660, it was now Cook who found himself on the wrong side of the law, and after an equally brief trial as that which the king received, Cook was also found guilty and was hanged, drawn and quartered on 16 October 1660, a phrase which will be explained in due course.

Compared to the fate that Cook received then, the king had been dealt with in a comparatively civilised manner by simply having his head removed in one nice clean cut, which ensured a still gruesome but presumably rather swift death. Cook, on the other hand, was first hanged almost to the point of death, which is the *hanged* part of the phrase. However, the most important word there, is almost, so we should very much remember that he was kept alive for the delights that were to come next.

Next, Cook had his penis and testicles removed, something that is termed emasculation. After that, a horizontal incision was made across his abdomen, after which his internal organs cascaded out in a squishy mess. Finally, and lastly, came the fun bit, for the executioner at least, where the body was quartered. Cook had his arms, legs and head removed, at which point he was declared well and truly and finally dead, and with a lot more certainty than Alice Blunden had been, that is for sure.

While this process might sound completely barbaric, the English were not necessarily completely uncivilised, however. For instance, this process would never have been carried out on a woman. Oh, no, like I said, we were not a completely uncivilised country back then. Women would simply be burned at the stake, alive.

And in a final salute to how civilised we have become as a country, the death penalty for treason remained a distinct possibility in England until 1998. The last person to be sentenced to death for treason had, in fact, been William Joyce, who was better known as Lord Haw-Haw, convicted in 1946, even though he was actually born an American and therefore, his defence counsel argued, owed no allegiance to the crown. Perhaps he should have thought about that, then, before he managed to obtain a British passport and had even voted in elections in the country. Joyce had also been a member of the British Union of Fascists and knew Oswald Mosley quite well. Incidentally, there is a common misconception that the death penalty still exists for treason in the UK, and I have heard this said many times by many people, but it is complete and utter bunkum.

We had decided to head for Lutterworth for a charge and consulted the map for the best way to go that would also take in one or two interesting places, but then realised that Lutterworth was our next destination anyway, and went straight for it.

Unfortunately, this would mean bypassing a place called Armourgeddon Military Museum, where for the princely sum of a few pounds, you can drive a tank or an armoured car or perhaps fire off a few shots at some pictures of the in-laws.

We headed for a supermarket in the town, where there was a fast charger according to Zap-Map, and were delighted to come across a roundabout on the outskirts of the town. For upon this roundabout was the life-sized model of the Gloster aircraft that Frank Whittle had built and flown from Gloucester and was the one I knew I had seen before, though I could not remember where. However, we should remember that the aircraft had only managed to reach an altitude of around five feet, so this sculpture with its depiction of the aeroplane soaring skywards does not quite tell the full story, but I shall let them off because it looked really good.

When we pulled up at the charger, we were dismayed to find it in use by someone in a BMW iX3. This dismay was because the batteries in those things are simply massive, compared to our tiny little Leaf anyway, and of course, the larger the battery is, the longer it takes to charge. Nonetheless, we pulled up, as we had no choice, really, though as I looked at the display on the charger, it told me that the charging process was almost complete after all. With that, a lady came back along with her two children, loaded in her shopping, and went.

Battery size is measured in kilowatt-hours. On the Leaf, this is 24-kilowatt hours, or kWh, which is why we have to charge every five minutes. As electric cars improve, they will obviously be able to travel further on a charge due to having larger batteries, and in addition to this, as more chargers are installed around the country, this will eventually lead to a better chance of getting a charge when you turn up somewhere. There is also a pattern that seems to be developing whereby if you want a rapid charge, you will have to pay for this luxury, but if you are happy with a slower charger, this is generally available for free at sites such as this supermarket. Whether the trend of free charging continues as more people adopt electric cars, however, remains to be seen, and it is conceivable that eventually, all charging will have to be paid for and that the current free charging options are merely carrots dangled in front of prospective electric car buyers intended to encourage them to make that purchase.

There are also, it has to be said, some practical benefits of having an electric car for current owners, such as the ability to use bus lanes in certain cities, free parking in others, and of course the fact that vehicle excise duty, more commonly known as road tax, is currently free. It is unlikely that these inducements will continue when there are twenty million of the things on the roads, so you cannot say you have not been warned.

I was discussing all of this with Rob, and I asked him if his next vehicle purchase is likely to be an electric one, and after not long at all, he told me that no, it would not. The reason, he added, was partly because of the issues we had encountered on this trip, and he said he would be a late adopter of this technology. He also said that the main reason was the initial cost of purchasing the car, which was quite simply unaffordable for him as things currently stood, as was probably the case for most people. I had only managed to get hold of my car at a reasonable price as I had bought at the right time, and I had bought a second-hand one.

With the car charged, we were now heading for a highlight of the day, and that was the village of Willey. There is nothing there, it is not famous for anything, and the only thing I could dig up about it that was even remotely interesting, other than its name, of course, was that the local pub, The Sarah Mansfield, had been renamed a few decades ago and had previously been known as The Plough. Why Sarah Mansfield? Well, that was the landlord's granny, of course. And by the way, if there was one place in England that should probably have a statue of a huge phallus, it is surely here and not Basingstoke. There was, however, not a single knob in sight unless, of course, you included Rob or myself.

As we sat before it, and in the hope of getting a drink, we were somewhat disappointed to find that the pub was shut. It was still relatively early in the day, so this was perhaps not all that surprising, but it actually appeared to be permanently closed. I would have loved to have spoken to the owner about the exact reason he renamed the pub, as I was certain that there was an interesting story there. Alas, it was not meant to be, so once again, we plodded on, this time to Pailton, just down the road.

We parked up just past a sign that read *The Baby Farm*, which was quite frankly a bit alarming and brought to mind crazy Victorian murderers, but then quickly realised that it was simply a shop that sold prams and the like, and was not some criminal underworld smuggling operation, at least not on the face of it.

Pailton was on our hit list because it had been the home of a man called Joseph Underhill, and I wanted to see exactly what the home of a man like him would be like because Underhill was a notorious miser who refused to spend any of his money and was in fact presumed to be very poor indeed.

I had seen a photo of Underhill, who had actually become known as the Pailton Miser, and he was a raggedy looking figure indeed. With torn and ripped clothes consisting of many layers, presumably to keep him warm, and sporting what looked like a wizard's hat as well as a long, matted beard, Underhill looked like one of Tolkien's hobbits, and who knows, maybe he was the inspiration for them?

The strange thing is that Underhill chose to live a miserly lifestyle and lived in a pigsty belonging to a Mrs Robins, rent-free, along with the pigs. The pigsty was opposite the Plough Inn, and I wondered if there were many Plough Inns around here and if that was why the licensee changed the name of his back in Willey, but that is a different story.

Anyway, Underhill had lived a relatively normal lifestyle in his early days, and had dressed smartly, and was even described as a *rustic dandy* by some. He was, however, bullied in his youth and rejected by women in adulthood, which may go some way to explaining his reclusive lifestyle. In his later years, he became known as *Old Joe* and must have been likeable, as there are several reports of people who tried to help him change his ways, though it seemed that he was happy in his pigsty. He lived there until he died in 1891 and quite surprisingly was found to have left £125 in his will, which is around £16,000 today. It is a mystery, then, why Underhill chose to live as he did.

The village, it turns out, is very nice. Fine buildings surround a village green, and 26 Coventry Road, where Old Joe lived, was just a short walk away. Unfortunately, it now appears to be a modern bungalow with a rather fetching palm tree in the garden, so I suspect we shall never know.

We were now heading for Astley Castle via Bedworth and would then head for Meriden in short order, which would mean driving a big arc around the north of Coventry. We had originally planned to stop in Bedworth, but quite frankly, we couldn't be bothered, sorry, Bedworth. We would have charged there at the local Tesco but simply didn't need to, so we continued on to Astley Castle, which was, in fact, much more interesting anyway.

We parked on a grass verge and walked down to the church, which is where we figured we would get the best view of the castle, and although it should really be considered a fortified manor house rather than a castle, castle does sound better, don't you think?

Whatever you want to call it, it dates back around 800 years to its origins, and though it has obviously changed over the centuries, it more or less gained its current form by 1500. At that time, it was owned by the Grey family, with perhaps the most famous member of the family, Lady Jane Grey, spending some of her life here. She later went down in history for being the monarch with the shortest reign and was on the throne for just nine days in July 1553, before being deposed by the rightful heir, her cousin Mary, though you may know her as Bloody Mary.

Lady Jane was then put on trial, for what it was, and after obviously being found guilty, she was swiftly executed. She was spared the usual sentence for a woman of being burned at the stake because of her position and instead had her head sliced off at the Tower of London, which can only really be classed as the lesser of two evils, and not necessarily a good thing.

The castle then sank into some obscurity, and not a lot of interest, to me at least, happened there until the Second World War. The army requisitioned the place, and it became a convalescent home for injured servicemen, but there were also other plans for the place, of the top-secret kind, that not even the army was aware of, well, not the British Army, anyway. For it is Astley Castle that none other than Adolf Hitler had his eyes on for a potential holiday home had he managed to invade our troublesome little island. It offered him a well-fortified and easily defendable structure, complete with its own moat, and was within easy commuting distance of all the major cities of the south, thereby helping him with his work-life balance, presumably. Thank goodness that never happened.

The church was nice enough and gave us good views of the castle, which was an odd combination of ancient structures seemingly interspersed with modern walls here and there. Someone had clearly done a good job of restoring the building and had decided to not mess about trying to rebuild it to make it look old. Instead, they had made a bold statement that said something like *yes, we know this bit looks modern but, hey, it's got wi-fi,* but anyway I liked it. I later found out that you can actually rent the place as a holiday home for a weekend if you have a thousand pounds or so to spare, which is much easier than invading a country to get it, you have to admit?

It was time for food, and what other place is there to get food than in the heart of England. I mean that in the most literal sense because we were now heading to Meriden, which was historically thought to be the geographical centre of England until we got decent maps, that is.

We parked in the large car park at the Bull's Head, which was surprisingly busy, and ventured inside to grab a table. Although it was a lot cooler today, I always prefer to sit inside a pub wherever possible so that I can eat my food without getting eaten by bugs, of which there were apparently more than a couple about today.

We perused the menu, which was alarmingly expensive, and we both decided to go for a dirty burger as it was one of the few items on the menu we could actually afford, to be honest. A couple of cokes would have to keep us going, as we could not afford another one, and while we waited for our food to come, we discussed our progress so far.

We were both still very much enjoying the trip, but despite our commitment to speed things up, we had, if anything, slowed down. Rather than make another decision to pull our fingers out, Rob suggested that we just go with the flow, and if we run out of time and have to go home, then so be it. We could always finish off the trip another time, and it would mean we would not have to miss any particular sections out, so we toasted our new recklessness and decided to carry on regardless.

When our burgers came, we found out that they were indeed very dirty, and enjoyed them very much. You get what you pay for, I thought, and this burger had been by far the nicest thing I had eaten so far and decided that as well as being reckless with time, I was now going to be reckless with money, at least when it came to food.

With full bellies, the waitress came over, and we got talking to her about Meriden, and she told us that the pub had a plaque marking the centre of England. In no time at all, she took us to see it, and we were delighted to find that there was also a map of England with directions to various UK cities, which featured none other than our home town of Hull. Ah, Meriden, the gift that keeps on giving, I thought to myself.

Conscious of the time, we paid our bill and wandered to the village green, where the waitress had also told us that there was a cross that marked the centre of England, though we figured it must be a different centre of England than was marked in the pub.

It was only a short walk, and lo and behold, we did indeed find a large ancient-looking cross, along with a plaque stating that it had marked the centre of England for some 500-years. Unfortunately, like so many things, this was complete and utter rubbish, and although Meriden was quite a nice place with a fine cross and a fantastic pub, one thing it was not was the centre of England. Those nice people at the Ordnance Survey have now clarified the matter and have decided that the centre of England actually lies 12-miles or so to the northeast at a place called Lindley Hill Farm and have placed yet another plaque there to prove it. I am glad to say that the farm is happily cashing in on this and now operate a campsite, and had we known when we passed it, we would have called in.

Our route would now take us around the south of Birmingham and then north past Wolverhampton, Stafford and Stoke, once again with some interesting stops along the way, but with the added advantage of having lots of electric chargers to choose from. We had no idea where we were going to stay tonight, but the weather promised rain, so we decided to just see how the afternoon went and headed for a place called Moseley Bogg.

It was only ten miles down the road but seemed as if it was a different world as we had entered a more urban type of area than we had been used to. For a moment, I wondered if this meant that we were now in the north of England, though I quickly dismissed this thought.

Moseley Bogg itself, however, was an oasis of

urban tranquillity, and as we followed walkways and platforms through the woods, we were transformed not back into the countryside but into some kind of fantasy realm. It may not surprise you, therefore, to learn that J.R.R. Tolkien grew up around here and that this place is yet another one that influenced his later works. He came here and was directly inspired to create the old forest in both The Hobbit and The Lord of the Rings, and walking around here, it was easy to see why.

The place is very popular with readers of those books, who now come from all over the world to see it, and half of them seemed to be here today, as we ducked and dodged between countless people along the narrow paths. There are also buzzards and woodpeckers, the former which we saw and the latter which we heard, and it was hard to imagine that we were actually in one of England's largest cities.

Moving on, we found King's Norton Stop Lock just four miles away, near Lifford Reservoir and not far from the watershed. We dumped the car, this time in a more suburban landscape, and took the short walk back to the canal.

The stop lock was exactly what it sounds like; it stops a canal, or more accurately, stops the water in that canal. This canal is called Kingswood Junction and joins the Stratford-on-Avon Canal with the Grand Union Canal. At the height of their use, different companies owned these canals, so the stop lock was built to stop one canal stealing water from the other.

The locks resemble two large guillotines, one on either side of the bridge, and together formed a small lock that allowed boats to travel from one canal to the other without allowing the theft of the water mentioned above. They were in use until the mid-20th century but are now left permanently open as all canals were nationalised in 1948, and the idea of theft became immaterial.

They are left open in the up position, which means that any passing canal boats have to pass under what is essentially, as already said, a very large guillotine, so we waited for a while to see a boat pass under on the off chance that the locks would fail and chop it in half. Sure enough, a brightly coloured little canal boat came chugging along but disappointingly made it through without being sliced in half.

I asked Robin if he wanted to go see Bella and find out who put her in the Witch Elm, but his blank look told me he didn't know what I was on about, so I explained in the car on the way.

I told him we were heading for Hagley to see the Wychbury Obelisk, but his face remained blank, and I began to wonder if he could hear me or if he had perhaps had a stroke. At the height of the Second World War, some local children made a gruesome discovery. While poaching in nearby Hagley

Wood, they found a human skull inside the hollow of a witch hazel tree, with a severed hand found nearby, which is an important point to remember. Obviously, the police were called, and they went on to find a complete skeleton, complete with dark hair and determined that it had been there for about eighteen months.

Because of the ongoing war, little headway was made on the case, and it began to fade into obscurity. However, in 1944, at least one person had not forgotten about the case, as graffiti appeared on a nearby abandoned building asking *Who put Luebella down the wych elm,* though the victim later came to be known as Bella.

Similar graffiti popped up around the area, including on the obelisk in Hagley, and it eventually became a famous part of local folklore. Over the years, various theories have been put forward suggesting that Bella was in fact either a local prostitute or a Nazi spy called Clara Bauerle after Clara's photo was found in the pocket of Josef Jakobs, the last man to be executed at the Tower of London after being captured spying for the Nazis. The prostitute theory is just that, and Clara Bauerle actually died in Berlin in 1942. Another theory suggested witchcraft, consistent with a ritual called the hand of glory, where a hand, usually a guilty hand that did some dastardly deed, is severed from the rest of a corpse at the time of death, as well as the fact that wych elms offered protection against witches, but the truth is that nobody really knows. Strangely, however, Bella's skeleton disappeared from storage. Several case files also mysteriously vanished, so it is certainly possible that something strange was going on, but once again, we shall probably never discover the truth.

When we arrived at the monument, we parked in the small car park at the bottom of the hill and felt some rain on the way up. There were plenty of people about, some walking their dogs and some just out for a stroll themselves, but all were enjoying the afternoon.

I am not ashamed to say that when we arrived at the top of the hill and saw the monument close up, I was a bit disturbed to find that it still had graffiti on it asking *who put Bella in the witch elm*, which sent a shudder through my body. Why anyone would want to continue to write this graffiti after so long made no sense to me, so we did not stay up there very long at all, although the view all around was absolutely amazing.

Deciding to go from one hollowed out tree to another, though one with a much more cheerful ending, we next decided to drive to Boscobel House via a Crooked House in Dudley, where we would charge both ourselves and the car.

This is the first time we had been stuck in what you could call traffic, and as we crept along road after road, apparently following our satnav on a magical mystery tour, we could at least be happy that we were not wasting any fuel at such low speeds.

We found a Costa coffee shop in Kingswinford for a rapid charge, giving up on getting a free charge nearby as it would take too long to walk to the Crooked House, but managed to overload on caffeine in the process.

Feeling as high as a kite, we drove to the Crooked House, and although it proved to be somewhat out of the way, we were instantly delighted that we had decided to come, as we had nearly knocked it off our list of things to see and places to go.

Have you ever come out of the pub, perhaps a little worse for wear, and discovered that the building looks a bit wonky? Well, the crooked house is like that even before you go in.

Built as a farmhouse in 1765, it became a pub in 1830 and has been entertaining people with its slippage ever since. This is no reflection on the builders, whoever they may be, but is a result of subsidence due to mining in the area over the last few centuries. As a result, the left walls of the pub stand around 4-feet lower than those on the right, which is quite a difference for any building, never mind one so small. The local council condemned the place after the war, but perhaps realising what a little gem of a place they had, the brewery spent a considerable sum of money building a metal frame to support the building, which not only makes it safe but protects its character too.

We went inside to grab a soft drink and a sit down, and the effect continues in there too. Walls meet each other at perilous angles, and windows are quite simply psychedelic. It was like wearing beer goggles.

The day was getting late, so we downed our cokes, which now gave us a sugar rush on top of the caffeine one, and jumped into the car to get to our final destination for the day, which was, of course, Boscobel House. Thankfully, the traffic had died down a little bit, though we still managed to arrive at Boscobel House just after they had closed.

This was not a problem, as we had not planned to go into the house as such anyway, but wanted to see a tree in the back garden. This might sound a bit odd, but it is an important part of English history and is as follows.

We have already heard of how Charles I was tried and executed in 1649, leaving the country without a monarch for the first time in its history. His son, also Charles and later to become Charles II, launched his first attempt at a comeback in 1650 but was beaten back and defeated at the Battle of Worcester. Forced to flee, Charles ended up here at Boscobel House after putting on a disguise and having his royal locks removed.

Brought into the house, he was given milk and small beer to refresh him, but with troops on the way, Charles had no option but to head into the woods and hide at the top of a hollowed-out oak tree that had been cut back some years earlier. He was in there for a full day and saw troops on the ground and all around him and knew full well that his fate, had he been found, would involve sharp things indeed.

When the troops left at dusk, Charles managed to return to the house, where he was well looked after, and finally managed to make his escape the next day. While at the house that night, he hid in a priest's hole, which is not as rude as it sounds but is, in fact, a secret compartment either beneath the floorboards or behind a wall. Lastly, if you have ever wondered where the name for any pub called The Royal Oak comes from, then it is from this incident.

It was perhaps better that the house had now closed, as this allowed us to follow the public footpath at the side of the house towards the oak tree and then jump over the fence as there was now nobody else around. The tree is protected and ringed by another fence and is obviously not the actual tree where the king hid, which was chopped up and stolen by souvenir hunters many moons ago. It is, however, in the same location and is a direct descendant of the original, so we still enjoyed our brief encounter with it, where we also managed to witness one of the most beautiful sunsets we had seen all year. We did not, however, have to jump any fences after all, as although the tree lies on private land, it does not belong to English Heritage, but is in fact owned by a nice farmer called Francis Yates who is quite happy to let all and sundry come and have a look at the tree completely free of charge, as long as you don't steal bits of it.

We had been sitting on a bench watching the sun go down, but intermittent showers promised fun times ahead. Rather than spending another night in a tent then, Robin suggested sharing the costs of a hotel, something which I agreed to immediately. With a couple of clicks of his phone, we were soon booked into a Premier Inn near Wolverhampton, where I am not ashamed to say I enjoyed getting out of my filthy clothes and into clean ones following a refreshing shower.

Wolverhampton is not famous for very much, I thought to myself as I got cleaned up, but then remembered that the town did give Portsmouth the FA cup just before the war, though I reckoned the local tourist authorities don't shout about that one very much. Once Rob had also managed to get himself tidied up a bit, we decided to do the only thing we could do, and we went into town to the Royal Oak pub, where we gave a toast to Charles II. Much later on, and on the way out of the pub, I remembered saying to Rob that it looked very much like the Crooked House.

THE UGLIEST VILLAGE IN ENGLAND

This morning was much more civilised than most as there was no drying of tents and repacking bags carefully into an over-crowded car, and all we had to do was to get dressed, which even I was capable of usually, and eat a full English breakfast, which I am something of an expert at, it has to be said.

As Robin and I discussed where we were going to go today, it is also probably a good time to discuss the elephant in the room that we completely failed to address yesterday, and that elephant is the sec-ond-largest city in the UK, also known as Birming-ham.

The watershed just happens to make an almost complete half-circle around the city, starting in the southeast near Meriden, all the way round in an anti-clockwise direction to Wolverhampton, where we were now. Although we do not, there-fore, need to go into the city as such, it is worth mentioning, if for no other reason than the hun-dreds of charging points dotted around it had we needed one.

But Birmingham has also given the world much more than this, although clearly there is far too much to tell than can fit on these humble pages. There are one or two things worth mentioning, however, and as we now live in a post-pandemic age, it is worth visiting the story of Janet Brown, a medical photographer at the University of Birmingham Medical School.

Birmingham, you see, has the unfortunate distinction of being the site of the last recorded smallpox outbreak. Scientists at a lab in the medical school, headed by Professor Henry Bedson, had been growing the virus in various Petri dishes and the like, but it appears that at some point, the virus escaped the laboratory (who would have thought?) and poor Janet Parker, who worked on the floor above, succumbed to the virus and died, going down in history with the dubious distinction of being the last recorded human being to die of it.

This was perhaps a little embarrassing to the World Health Organisation, which had just spent the week preparing a press-release announcing the eradication of the disease. They immediately descended on Birmingham in large numbers fearing a larger outbreak, fears which were incredibly justified as the disease had already killed 300 million people in the 20th century alone.

Everyone was on edge for the next twelve days or so, as that is the incubation period for smallpox, and anyone who had had even the slightest contact with Janet was given a vaccination, which amounted to some 500 people. The source of the outbreak was quickly identified, and when it finally became evident that no more instances of the disease would be found, everyone was able to relax a little.

There were, however, two more deaths that were directly related to the outbreak. Janet Brown's father died of a cardiac arrest which was thought to have been caused by the stress he suffered as a result of his daughter's illness, and Professor Bedson, who had been in charge of the laboratory, killed himself on the same day that Parker died, probably as a result of the guilt he felt over the whole affair. He left a suicide note confirming this, stating *I am sorry to have misplaced the trust which so many of my friends and colleagues have placed in my work.*

On what is, quite frankly, not much of a better note, Birmingham was also the site of one of the strongest tornados ever to have hit the British Isles. This happened in July 2005, causing estimated damages of around £40 million and was probably around F3 on the Fujita scale, which is used to measure the power of a tornado, where F5 represents the most powerful.

Bizarrely, tornados are not all that uncommon in the UK, and Theodore Fujita, who obviously invented the scale that bears his name, even goes so far as to say that the UK receives the highest number of tornadoes in relation to its land area than any other country in the world.

And finally, on this note, it is actually Portsmouth, which is, of course, where we started our little trip, that holds the record for the strongest tornado to have ever hit our little island. Way back in December 1810, a tornado struck Southsea in the town and damaged and even completely levelled numerous houses, with the roof of a local bank being *rolled up like a piece of canvas.*

I know that those two things are perhaps just a little negative, so in the interests of balance, I am also going to say that Birmingham gave us lots of good stuff, such as UB40 and Duran Duran, for which I thank it very much and promise to shut up about it.

Our first job today was to top the car up, which we did without trouble just down the road at the Moreton Arms, after which we got back on track and carried on from where we left off. We drove past Boscobel House, which was still well and truly closed due to the early hour, and continued to Bishops Wood, where we pulled up outside the Royal Oak pub.

Of course, the car park was empty given the time of day, and we had only stopped here for a single reason. As we walked to look at the front of the pub, we could see that it was clearly an old building. This was to be expected, as this pub was, in fact, the very first to bear the name of The Royal Oak, named after the tree at nearby Boscobel House. Unfortunately, I could not see a date anywhere on the building. There was no one to ask, so after a minute or two, we decided to move on and look for something more exciting.

We settled on Norbury, a few miles to the north, and parked on a lane near the church. The church itself proved to be fantastic and reminded me of the Houses of Parliament, as grand as it was. Fancy tombs signified the final resting places of Sir Henry Fitzherbert and Ralph and Nicholas, whoever they were, although they had clearly had a lot of money at some point.

This was not why we were here, though, so as we ventured outside to have a look around, I told Robin about Richard Barnfield, who had been born here in the 1500s to a family of some standing. Barnfield had attended Oxford, after which he began to publish poetry. He was way ahead of his time, although he encountered problems with his first volume, as some of his poetry had clearly homosexual tendencies, something many regarded as taboo at the time.

Facing considerable criticism, when he published his second set of works, he started it with a bold statement that distanced himself from his previous work and acknowledged that some may have misinterpreted the story of love between a shepherd and a boy. He was, however, probably poking fun at his critics, as his new volume was *explicitly and unashamedly homoerotic and full of physical desire*, according to one of the very critics that had previously had a go at him.

So it is then that Barnfield led his life poking fun at those around him but in a very clever way, and he gained such a reputation that it is said that none other than Shakespeare himself considered Barnfield to be his closest rival poet. Until this trip, I had never even heard of Barnfield, but then I was never all that much interested in Shakespeare; but had Shakespeare not lived, it is likely that we would today hold Barnfield in the high regard of that of the bard himself.

This is an odd thought, as whether or not you are interested in Shakespeare and whether or not you think you can quote any of his work, I can guarantee that even though you are probably not, you probably can if you know what I mean. His work, you see, has permeated the English language so much that a lot of our modern-day English is based on what he wrote hundreds of years ago.

For instance, if you've ever sent someone packing, broken the ice, eaten your parents out of house and home or been in a pickle, then you've quoted Shakespeare. It does not stop there, though. If you've ever had too much of a good thing, worn your heart on your sleeve or been on a wild goose chase, then these too come directly from Shakespeare. Who knew? Not me, that's for sure.

Norbury was nice, but there was not much else here, so it was soon time to move on. We found our way along winding lanes and through rolling fields and dark woods, finally coming to the village of Woodseaves. We parked just before the village in a layby next to a bridge that passes over the Shropshire Union Canal, beneath which was said to lie a true oddity. Underneath the bridge, you see, is the fabled smallest telegraph pole in Britain. I was keen to get a photo of my good friend Rob, who is, of course, a giant of a man (compared to me at least) simply because I thought this would be funny.

We walked down the embankment to the canal but could find no sign of the telegraph pole, so we decided to walk underneath the bridge to the other side. Still unable to see it, we thought we would walk a bit further, but after a few minutes of disappointment, we decided to cut our losses and return to the car.

As we turned around, we saw the pole, which had been hidden immediately beneath the bridge but above an extra arch that had been added to increase the strength of the structure. This, unfortunately, meant that we could not get a picture with Rob standing next to and probably towering above the pole. For some reason, he was reluctant to risk his life climbing up the bridge, the spoilsport.

We had no choice, then, but to risk life and limb another way. Our next stop was the small village of Ashley, just a twenty minute drive away. Parking outside the church, which is exactly where we wanted to be, we wandered off to find what was supposed to be a burial mound from the time of the black death. We found it in almost no time at all, in fact, we could see it from the cemetery behind the church, and I made a mental note not to do any digging. After being a bit underwhelmed with the pile of mud, we wandered into the church to examine the many fine sculptures of rich people, most of which looked like William Shakespeare, it has to be said.

Because we have attention spans similar to monkeys, Rob and I had soon had enough of the church and yearned for something else. We decided that today had been the least exciting day so far and longed for something to brighten it up a little, and as we were getting a little hungry, with our breakfast now seeming a million miles ago, we decided to head into Newcastle-under-Lyme for some fast food, as well as a fast charge.

We found a rapid charger at a local supermarket and went off to find something edible, which we stumbled across at Dixy Chicken, and I sincerely hope I don't have to explain to you what we ate. According to the little sticker in the window, the place had a five-out-of-five score, and after devouring my bargain-bucket, I was more than happy.

Newcastle was slightly off the line of the watershed, which ran around the town to the northwest, so we didn't stay long, preferring to hit the road again in search of interesting places to stop, but I often wondered how much of a chip on their shoulders do the people that live here have? For instance, if you buy a ticket from anywhere in the country to Newcastle, there is no chance you will end up here, but will instead stumble out of a train station in the frozen northeast of England. If you want to come here then, you would have to be very specific and remember to say the whole of the town's name, which would surely get very annoying very quickly? I do sympathise a little, as the proper name for my little town is Kingston-upon-Hull, though of course, nobody calls it that. If you mention Kingston, then everyone assumes you mean the place near London, and if you say Hull, well, no-one knows where that is either. On a positive note, my home town is pretty quiet, and I would even go so far as saying it is an undiscovered gem, basically because nobody can find it.

Anyway, it was time to move on, and although the traffic of Newcastle slowed our exit somewhat and almost seemed to be trying to keep us here, we headed for Halmer End, which was just four miles away.

We parked outside the pub, The Railway, and walked to the edge of the village where we found a memorial to what had happened here over one hundred years ago, which had been a coal mining disaster of epic proportions. I had heard of the Minnie Pit Disaster but could not have told you anything about it other than many people had died.

The mine was first sunk in 1881 and was an incredibly profitable venture for the owner, who had named it after his daughter, apparently, so I sincerely hope she was called Minnie.

There had, however, been one or two incidents, and the mine became known for containing dangerous gases that had killed all of the pit ponies in 1898 but thankfully, no men, though another explosion in 1915 killed 9 men. Furthermore, the death toll had been so low on both of these occasions for one purely random occurrence – both had occurred on Sundays.

Fast-forward to 1918 and the closing days of the First World War, and demand for coal was as high as ever. On Saturday 12th January, and on what would have been an otherwise normal day for the 248 men down the mine at the time, a huge explosion ripped through the workings, killing 155 men. Search teams scoured the pit for survivors, pulling many out alive, although one rescuer was later killed, taking the death toll to 156.

The loss of 156 men from this area was an incredible price that the local community could not afford to pay, and it has to be remembered that this was on top of the many men who had been killed in the trenches of France at the same time. Many families had lost their main wage earner and lived in poverty from then on, despite compensation being paid to affected families, which quite simply wasn't enough. As the economy deteriorated further, the pit was finally forced to close in 1930, having never fully recovered from the events of that fateful Saturday.

I read all this at the memorial that marked the event, which is in a nature reserve on land reclaimed after the mine closed, and which paid tribute to all those who lost their lives in the fight to extract coal from this mine. The word fight is important here, as it should be remembered that being a miner was never the safe option, even when compared to being sent to fight in a war.

On one of the information boards, there was a picture that was credited to an individual named George Bissill, and my mind flashed back to the dog walker we had met who had told me to visit Ashmandsworth and to find out about a man called George Bissill, but due to problems with the car that day, we had not quite made it.

The picture was a very graphic representation of a miner, who seemed almost oversized as a human, and was clearly one of those government propaganda posters that had been so popular in the distant past.

It turns out then that this George Bissill was the same as the one that had come from Ashmandsworth, and he had, in fact, started life as a miner. During the First World War, he had joined the army as a way to escape an underground life but had then been cruelly appointed to a company of sappers and miners, whose job it was to dig tunnels, of course.

Anyhow, he survived the war, though he did not come through it unscathed, being injured in an accident on one occasion and gassed during combat in another. Awarded a pension for his injuries, this did at least allow him to pursue life as an artist, and the rest, as they say, is history. Much of his work focused on mining and is perhaps quite dark, but he also painted some brighter works later, when he was presumably somewhat recovered from his wartime experiences.

I suggested to Rob that we try to find something a bit more cheerful to do, as stories about the black death and mining accidents were not exactly making us laugh, which is how we ended up at a pub called The Foxhound on the edge of Biddulph Moor, in search of the source of the River Trent, the third-longest river in England.

We had apparently hit the jackpot with this pub, and we realised as soon as we caught sight of it that it was something special, for in the garden was a giant pedalo in the shape of a swan, even though there wasn't a lake in sight. That wasn't all either, as once we had parked up, we also found a pink flamingo, a gorilla, an elephant and even E.T. -

the extra-terrestrial.

We went inside to grab a pint of coke each and came back out to find a picnic table, but the place appeared to be busy today, and they were all taken. It was then I suggested to Rob that we sit in the pedalo instead, and for some reason, he asked me if I meant the flamingo or the swan.

I wasn't particularly bothered, which is how on a hot summer afternoon, we found ourselves sipping a nice cold drink in a swan-shaped pedalo about as far from the sea in England as you could get, which is not a circumstance that I would have ever have concocted, to be honest. Yes, we did get a few strange looks, and no, we did not really fit into the pedalo, especially Robin, but it was a nice day, and we were happy, which was all that matters.

The actual source of the river is not a specific spring, so to speak, but is the whole of Biddulph Moor, which is just behind the pub and is what we were currently sat staring at, so I mentioned to Robin that we had done a fine job of finding the source of the river, and sarcastically mentioned what hard work it had been. He concurred, he told me, and said that we deserved another drink, as well as a packet of crisps, which he promptly popped off to get.

The Trent, then, at around 189-miles long, goes from here and drains most of the midlands towards Nottingham and then on to the Humber Estuary, where it passes my house on its way to the North Sea. As I sat waiting for Rob to return, I wondered how long it takes for water to get from here to the sea, and although I guessed that this was longer than you might expect, I figured I would never know the answer, but never mind.

We sat there for quite some time, being completely lazy and drinking and eating things that were not necessarily good for our bodies, but finally, and somewhat reluctantly, we decided to move on.

Funnily enough, the heavens opened up as we got in the car, which was a problem as my window was wide open once again. By the time I had repeatedly pressed the button to slowly force it to shut, two things had happened – I had become totally soaked, and it had stopped raining once again.

We headed next to Gradbach, where we would visit another church, although this time, one with a difference. We found the village soon enough, parked in the empty car park, and started the short walk up to it.

Passing a youth hostel and clopping over a foot-bridge, a sign pointed us towards Swythamley and up a hill, somewhere near the top of which we would find the church.

We met a few people coming the other way, and one of them confirmed that we were going in the right direction when they saw us studying a map, and we were soon there.

Lud's Church is not, however, anything built by man. You could say it was built by God if you wanted to because the church is a work of nature and is incredibly beautiful.

It is, in fact, a natural chasm with walls covered in lush moss. As we entered the shadows within, the temperature dropped considerably, and it was much cooler in there than it had been outside. It felt like another world, with an almost fairy-tale appearance, particularly at this time of year, which was, of course, the height of summer.

The walls rose 60-feet on either side of us, and we followed the contours of the chasm, enjoying the cool breeze that blew over us.

It is said that it was used as a secret place of worship in the 15th century, hence the church part of the name, but it also has other deep links to history. It is said to be here where Robin Hood took refuge at one point, along with his merry men, and it is also supposed to be the place that inspired the *Green Chapel* in the legend of King Arthur.

Whether any of that was true or not, I did not know, but what Robin and myself both agreed on was that this was one of the most beautiful places we had seen on this journey, and we loved every minute we spent there, which was quite frankly not long enough.

We returned to the car, and with it, the oppressive heat of the day, to head towards Buxton, where we could top the car up before deciding where to camp that night. On the way, though, we drove through Flash, which is the highest village in the UK. This fact really surprised me, as you would have thought that the highest village would surely have been somewhere in Scotland.

Unfortunately, the drive up to the village had taken its toll on the battery, and as a result, the sat-nav gave us an alarming message that we did not really want to hear, which was that we might not have enough range to make it to our destination.

Since the beginning of the journey, where we had encountered several difficulties related to charging, and we had, of course, run out of miles on just one occasion, we had actually been doing rather well, and we thought we had got the hang of managing the miles, so we figured that the next few might be a bit tricky, but had no option than to plough on anyway.

Flash itself was nice enough, though we dared not stop. We did note that the height of the village, however, was 1,519 feet. This is higher than its nearest competition, Wanlockhead in Scotland, but this is disputed by the Scots, who claim their village is higher.

Anyway, we carried on, and with Robin navigating, I advised him that now was not the time to get his left mixed up with his right, so I helpfully wrote him a note that he could stick on top of the glove box to help him out. He was not amused, and he merely crumpled my note and tossed it in the back, so I told him that when we become stranded in the countryside and either die of starvation or get eaten by the locals, it's all on him.

Luckily, the roads began to hint at certain downhill tendencies, and a strange thing happens when you drive an electric car down a hill, you gain range. The car regenerates electricity back into the battery through the very motors that power it uphill, so once again, we figured that the computer estimating our range simply could not be trusted. Before long, we had gained not one mile but five, and we were once again happy and confident in our ability to get to Buxton.

We had a surprisingly large choice of chargers in Buxton and chose the supermarket because it had both a fast charger and an air-conditioned building, or maybe even a freezer to crawl into. And although Buxton was not exactly on the watershed, it was as close as it was possible to get to around here, with the actual watershed running past the town just a mile or two to the northwest.

I had been to Buxton many times, though I would not say I knew it well, but could vouch that it was a very nice place. The Victorians clearly thought his too, and it became a spa-town where rich people could go to bathe, and it is, in fact, England's highest market town, at the dubiously specific figure of exactly 1,000 feet above sea level. Part of its success as a spa-town is because the water emerges from the ground here at the decidedly balmy and extremely agreeable temperature of 28° Celsius. It has enjoyed further success in modern times as the ideal place from which to explore the Peak District, which is named not after the peaks that make up the landscape but is actually a corruption of the Picts, the peoples that once inhabited the area, which is something that had never occurred to me.

It had also known notoriety recently when the local police force decided to dye the waters of a local beauty spot, known as the Blue Lagoon, black, to dissuade visitors during what was supposed to be a time of lockdown due to COVID-19, for which they obtained considerable negative publicity. However, the fact is that the police knew something that the holidaymakers didn't, which is the true nature of the Blue Lagoon. It is an old quarry with the waters being a toxic soup of chemicals, carcases, and other detritus of the modern age and is probably the last place you would ever want to go for a swim.

The town itself is very nice, though, with lots of fancy old buildings, and it was clearly very popular with tourists today as we found out when we had a short walk around the place.

With the car fully charged, however, there was no reason for us to stay in such a nice little place, so it was off to the ugliest village in Britain we went next, and that is why we ended up in Dove Holes.

Now, I am not sure who voted this village as such, but ugliness was clearly not the impression we both had when we parked up at the train station. Sure, it might not win any awards for being Britain's most beautiful village, but the ugliest village it certainly was not, although it was in dire need of a bypass, having a major road running right through the heart of the place.

However, it was the train station that we had come to find and was only on our list because of something that had happened here a couple of years back. Lewis Capaldi, famous rock legend, of course, filmed the video for his song *Someone You Love* right here in Dove Holes, or more specifically at the train station where we now stood. In the video, in which Lewis has managed to persuade his dad's cousin, Doctor Who, also known as Peter Capaldi, to star (nothing wrong with a bit of nepotism, I will star in a rock video any time my children ask me to) Capaldi senior plays the seemingly very sad role of a husband who has lost his wife.

As the video goes on, however, it turns out that his wife has also donated her organs, specifically her heart, to save the life of another. The other in question then turns out to be a wife and mother herself, and we also see that prior to meeting her at the end of the video, Capaldi had unknowingly passed her in the street while having no idea who she was.

This is now one of my favourite songs and videos.

If I was an actor and needed to get the tears flowing in double-quick time, all I would have to do is watch this video. I would start crying at exactly one minute, forty-three seconds when Capaldi meets the lady and her family.

Maybe I'm just a softy, or maybe it's because my family have been through something similar ourselves, I do not know. My son received a solid organ transplant when he was just a young boy, and we have not yet managed to get in touch with the donor family. Why this is, I am not sure. Perhaps we are scared or do not wish to revisit the past, but whatever the reason, I think of this every time I see my son and quietly thank whoever made this possible.

Wiping away the tears, so Rob does not see, we both agree that this place is not at all bad, but nonetheless, off we go, this time just a short hop to the interestingly named Chapel-en-le-Frith, which more or less means chapel in the forest, and on the way, we pass through another place with a strange name, this one being Sparrowpit. We only come this way because the watershed dissects the village almost perfectly at a pub called *The Wanted*, a most unusual name for a pub, though we do not stop as there is very little here and the pub is shut.

Arriving in Chapel-en-le-Frith and once again choosing to park in a supermarket, we use a standard speed charger rather than a rapid one as the battery is far from empty. We decide to top it up anyway as we think that there may be fewer chargers available for the next few miles due to the rural nature of the landscape. It will also get quite hilly, which we expect will take more out of the battery, and after all, we don't want to have to use the breakdown service again. It's not that I am afraid of Mick, well, maybe just a little bit.

While the car is charging, we walk along the high street to the marketplace to look at the old stocks previously used to punish petty criminals. I am reminded of the good old days when you could just beat criminals and throw rotten vegetables at them, and I find myself thinking how much I actually miss the 1980s.

The stocks are interesting, but unfortunately, it does not seem possible to mess with them to get an incriminating photo of Robin but never mind. Interestingly, this spot is also the exact spot where Will Scarlet, faithful friend of Robin Hood, died on a cold and wintry day back in December 1283, after a battle with the sheriff's men. Interestingly, Little John, another staunch ally of Robin Hood, is said to be buried just east of here at Hathersage, though neither claim is proven. In the case of Little John, the claim is centred around the discovery of a single thigh bone, upon which analysis also states that he was over 8-feet tall, which is even bigger than my good friend Rob.

Moving on, and with the clouds having moved in with the welcome effect of cooling us down, we head west to a place that may well sound familiar to you. This is Whaley Bridge and has recently become rather famous, although not necessarily for the right reasons.

In the late summer of 2019, heavy rain and flooding caused severe damage to Toddbrook Reservoir, which is just at the south-western edge of the town and which had been happily holding water back since 1832. Events soon escalated, and things became very dramatic indeed when it seemed that the dam really was about to burst and flood the town, which would not have been the best outcome, according to one local resident. Television crews arrived and broadcast footage of RAF Chinook helicopters dramatically lifting in countless sandbags to save the houses below. At the same time, pumps attempted to lower the water level to take the strain from the already failing dam wall.

We parked at The Cock, this one being a pub and not having the slightest resemblance to a phallus, and followed a footpath over a river and towards the reservoir, getting there in good time. We may or may not have hopped over a couple of fences that we possibly shouldn't have, but please don't copy us as we are mere children at heart, you see.

We find the reservoir rather empty, and figure that work is still ongoing to figure out how to repair it, and at the same time see two professional-looking types in jeans and hard hats scratching their chins and looking at a large blueprint which appears to be upside down, which does not exactly instil us with confidence.

We also notice that there are rather a lot of houses downstream from the reservoir; in fact, the whole town of Whaley Bridge appears to be so, and I cannot help but wonder what has happened to property prices here lately. I cannot imagine anyone wanting to move here under the current conditions and decide to have a quick look to see how much they are going for. They do appear to be competitively priced, I find, and I am amused to find the description of one stating that it is handy for the swimming pool. I'll bet.

As it is getting late in the day, and as we cannot afford a luxury night in a hotel like we did the previous night, Robin searches for a campsite as I drive us to our next destination of Hayfield, halfway between Whaley Bridge and Glossop.

Unfortunately, we find ourselves once again stuck behind a rather large tractor, although once again, we take comfort in the fact that this will probably allow us to cover more miles. Still, it is frustrating that it takes us almost forty minutes to cover ten miles but never mind.

There must be something going on in Hayfield, either that or the people are really cheerful, as bunting hung everywhere. We wander up to the Royal Hotel but decide it is too expensive for us, and cross the bridge to look at the church.

The church has an interesting history, sort of, as this is where a zombie outbreak occurred in 1745. At the end of August, the minister of another church back at Chapel-en-le-Frith is said to have witnessed hundreds of bodies rising from the graves here at St Matthew's. He may have been at the brandy, of course, or he may have just been trying to give what was essentially a rival church a bad name, but whatever happened, there were no other witnesses.

The 1700s was perhaps a spooky time to live around here because just a few years later, in 1760, a witch by the name of Suzannah Huggin was said to be up to mischief. She sold a charm to an old sailor, and when he promptly vanished, and she was found to once again be in possession of the charm, she was taken to the local pub and pelted with rotten fruit and then almost stoned to death. The charm became synonymous with bad luck, and eventually, it had to be exorcised by the local clergy.

On a brighter note, we next wandered to see the birthplace and presumably childhood home of none other than Captain Mainwaring, real name Arthur Lowe, and we stopped for a photo opportunity in front of the blue plaque that now sits on the front of 63 Kinder Road, much to the bemusement of the window cleaner who was currently there but must have somehow mistaken the windows for port-holes on a ship and was busy concentrating on cleaning only a circle in the centre of each pane of glass.

We soon got talking to him when he offered to take both our pictures together, and when we told him what we were doing, he gave us an interesting bit of information about Kinder Scout, which was the hill just to our east, and the mass trespass of 1932 which I was already somewhat familiar with. However, the interesting bit was when he told us that the trespass actually started at Bowden Bridge Quarry, just next to the bridge, though it was now flooded and had become a pool. We thanked him for this and decided to walk up the lane just to have a look at this little piece of history, and as we stood at the edge of the pool, I wondered about all of those brave individuals that took part, some of whom also took a beating, and that without them we would not be able to wander in the countryside as freely as we do today.

As we walked back down the hill to the car, clouds moved over and started to rain on us, and although it was not a heavy downpour, we were pretty wet by the time we got back there.

We had not dried out by the time we had driven to Chunal, just a couple of miles down the road, and although we had intended to have a wander around, we just sat in the car listening to the patter of raindrops hitting the roof.

The sight we were looking at would probably not

have changed much since a guy called Ludwig Wittenstein lived here in the early 1900s. Although Ludwig was technically a philosopher, with some considering him to be the greatest philosopher of the 20th century, for some reason, he spent his time here flying aeronautical kites in the upper atmosphere during thunderstorms.

Ludwig had inherited a lot of money when he was very young, and while this gave him the freedom to do whatever he wanted, which clearly included trying to electrocute himself, the First World War saw him serving on the frontlines, which must have been difficult, to say the least. He suffered severe depression after the war and became a teacher, but he had a bad habit of beating his pupils, with this culminating in him knocking a young boy unconscious in 1926, landing him in court.

Luckily his wealthy background made the matter quickly disappear, though it still clearly troubled Ludwig, as he revisited the boy ten years later to ask for forgiveness. Ludwig eventually gave most of his fortune to his brothers and sisters, which didn't necessarily help them, and three of his brothers committed suicide, which must have further driven Ludwig into depression. Seeming almost tired of life and conscious that other people could neither understand nor appreciate his work, when a doctor told him he was going to die, he simply said *Good,* and that was the end of that.

Robin told me that this was a very depressing story and that I should not include it, but, well, here it is, and you are welcome.

With the rain not looking like it would stop any time soon, we finished off the last bit of the drive to Glossop and plugged the car in at a rapid charger in a Lidl car park. I wondered aloud to Robin about how many fines were going to drop through my letterbox in a couple of weeks, as we had not necessarily bought anything from all of the stores we had visited, but he reminded me that we were paying good money for this electricity and that anyone who sent one was free to shove their fine where the sun doesn't shine.

The sun certainly wasn't shining in Glossop, not today at least, so it was in the Norfolk Arms that we spent the next hour or so where I am not ashamed to say I had not only a starter and a main course, but a pudding too. It was a tidy little pub, with nice wood panelling adorning the walls, and the service was both incredibly quick and friendly. Our waiter, Jamie, earned his tip that night simply by telling us that famous artist LS Lowry was buried in the town, but he also directed us to a fantastic little campsite at Crossgate Farm. Furthermore, when we arrived at the campsite, the rain was gone, and as it was almost dark and our bellies were full, we both slept like babies almost as soon as we climbed into our tents.

THE GOOD SAMARITAN

We actually slept in this morning and were awakened by the sounds of clanging pans, and hushed voices at around 7am. I shouted to Robin that we were late but heard only a muffled grunt in return, so I stayed in my cosy sleeping bag for a few minutes more.

Finally summoning up the willpower to go and have a look outside, I found a dreary and drab day greeting me, and as I stretched my arms and legs in my usual morning routine, I noticed that the car, which was parked a short distance away, had a flat tyre, and my heart sank.

Presumably, in order to save weight, or perhaps money if I were a cynic, the manufacturers had decided that the little Leaf did not need a spare tyre, which is something I can generally vouch for. In almost forty-thousand miles of driving in this little motor, I had not had a single tyre-related incident, although always at the back of my mind was what I would do when the inevitable happened. I was aware of a small can of gunk hidden somewhere in a secret compartment in the boot, and as I rifled through the back of the car looking for it, I was reminded of the soldiers looking for King Charles hidden in the priest hole at Boscobel House. My incident was a lot less exciting, though, and the political ramifications for the future of England are, admittedly, slightly less severe.

I found the tin, as well as an air compressor, and declined to read the instructions as I find that I have made it this far through life without doing so, and I wasn't going to start doing that sort of thing at my age. I screwed the hose on the tyre and was just about to let rip when a voice from behind me told me to just try to pump the tyre up first, as it was probably only a slow puncture when you consider that we managed to drive in here last night.

This was Glen, who was pitched up next to us, and he said he was a mechanic, so I took his advice if only because I did not know what I was doing. Unfortunately, the tyre proceeded to deflate almost as fast as it went up, so I gave up on the idea of trying to limp back into town with it and once again grabbed the can of gunk.

Glen was not keen for me to do this, however, and he explained that once you have used that stuff on the tyre, it is rendered useless after a few miles of driving, and it cannot ever be repaired. He went down on his knees and seemed to be sniffing the tyre as it slowly hissed towards flatness once again, which I thought odd, but then he announced that he had found it, whatever it was, and got back up again.

After he had helped me empty the boot of our remaining gear, which was now unceremoniously dumped in a scruffy pile on the damp grass, Glen had jacked the car up and removed the wheel and was now beckoning me to come with him to find a garage. It was still pretty early, so I'm not sure where we were heading at this unearthly hour, but just a few minutes later, we were at Glossop Tyres, and a young man was doing all manners of things to my wheel even though they were technically still not open.

Glen was apparently very persuasive and had told the young lad about our journey up the middle of the country, and in no time at all, he had repaired the tyre and rebalanced it, whatever that means, but then refused to accept any payment.

It was not until we were back at the campsite with Glen tightening up the wheel that I realised Robin was still nowhere to be seen, so after we had given the wheel one final check and, once I had promised Glen his five minutes of fame within these pages, I did the only thing I could, and went over and kicked his tent.

A muffled groan came from within, and I told him to get up as we were late and waited for him to come out. It was like watching a bear come out of hibernation on the first day of spring, as he slowly and methodically crawled out on all fours and then forced himself up skywards. A stretch that was far more impressive than mine reminded me of the five stages of man, where we are seen to evolve from an ape to a modern human, similar to one of those charts that we have all seen either at school or in a textbook. I got the impression that Rob never quite completed the last stage, judging by his demeanour this morning anyway, and I was also reminded that one in every two-hundred men are direct descendants of Genghis Khan.

As Robin slowly became aware of his surroundings, he threw me a reluctant greeting of good morning and then turned to the car and asked why all of our stuff was on the floor. It must have been a rhetorical question as he then stumbled off to the toilet block, so I didn't bother replying, and I decided not to tell him that I had been up for over an hour sorting the tyre out.

We finally left the campsite and headed east along a pretty road that took us to Crowden, and we had spectacular views over the valleys and reservoirs to the south. There must have been a slow truck up ahead that was presumably struggling with the gradient as well as the twisting road, but despite being late, we were still in no hurry, even though technically we had to at least start thinking about heading home tomorrow.

We passed several isolated cottages and houses along the way, and I felt jealous every time we did so, as I would absolutely love to come and live out here in the fresh air and under big skies. I imagined this would be a good place to sit and look at the stars at night, and then realised that although we had been given this opportunity every night this week, we had not done so as we had been so tired. I had ventured out once or twice in the night for reasons that you do not want to know, and I had certainly seen a few stars then, but this is not the same as staying out purely for that purpose, so I vowed to do so tonight.

Crowden had a car park and a campsite, and after treating us to a nice healthy breakfast in the form of ice cream, we had a wander to the church and back, which was pleasant and allowed us to stretch our legs. It looked like the place would be busy with walkers today, and I can understand why, as the hills around here clearly offered some good walking routes.

It was back in the car for us, though, and as we continued east, we found ourselves heading towards Woodhead Pass, an infamous road that is often closed in the wintertime but one that has also been voted one of the best driving experiences in the country. Robin told me that this road had even been the subject of a song, *The Snake*, written by the Human League, who suggested this road as an alternative to the motorway. I didn't believe him, but when I later tried to fact-check him solely for the reason of pulling him up on it, I discovered that he was, in fact, correct. I never said anything, as I didn't want to give him the satisfaction of knowing he was right, so I kept quiet, as that's what friends are for, right?

Woodhead Reservoir itself was stunningly beautiful, though the water level was markedly low as it usually is at this time of year. It has been here for over one hundred and fifty years and was the first reservoir around here that those industrious Victorians started work on, though it was the last to be completed. We have driven past a few reservoirs today, six in fact, which are all part of the same chain, with Woodhead being the highest one. The lowest one, Arnfield Reservoir, nearest Manchester, is actually linked to the city with a 6-foot diameter tunnel, which carries a staggering 50-million gallons of water a day, and when I thought about this, I decided that I needed the loo.

We turned off from the main road at this last reservoir and headed north, ultimately towards Holmfirth, where we intended to charge again. We reckoned we had lost most of our worries regarding range in the little Leaf, as we figured that we now had a very good idea of how far we could get on a charge, so we were not worried when we started heading up several steep hills and saw our alleged range plummet on the dashboard of the car.

This part of the route was also stunning, despite today's inclement weather. Dark and forbidding clouds hung above the moors all around us, but this only added an air of drama to the scenery, which was incredibly beautiful in any weather.

We caught glimpses of a few more reservoirs, and as we crested the top of the heather-clad moors, we saw ahead of us the town of Holmfirth, far below us on the valley bottom. It was a long, gentle drive down a very big hill, which saw the range of the Leaf increase once more, which I took advantage of by changing from one driving mode to another to make full use of the regeneration, where the car uses surplus electricity to put energy back into the traction battery.

The two modes are drive and eco, and eco is the one that regenerates more power to the battery, but it causes the vehicle to slow quicker, almost acting as a brake. In the drive mode, regeneration still occurs but at a much slower rate, meaning there is less drag on the car, and it seems to coast along more efficiently. I only really put the car into eco on the bends and tried to avoid using the brake wherever possible. By doing this, the range of the car had increased by an amazing ten miles by the time we drove into Holmfirth a short while later.

The watershed technically runs a few miles to the southwest of the town, but there are no roads there, so we had no choice but to come this way. However, this is good news as Holmfirth just happens to be one of my favourite places and is best known as the filming location for the classic comedy series *Last of the Summer Wine*.

I grew up with this little gem of a programme but only really bothered with the first few series featuring the original cast of Compo, Clegg and Foggy, three geriatric friends who get up to all sorts of mischief in this little Yorkshire town and the surrounding countryside, which kind of reminds me of myself and my mates. The series went on to become the world's longest-running sitcom, going on for a staggering 37 years, a title that it still holds today and will for some time longer, I expect.

We headed to the main car park in the centre of town, where there was a rapid charger, but unfortunately found that it was occupied already, and after consulting our trusty map, we discovered that our only other options were all what we would consider slow chargers. Given that we had no choice, we ended up at a supermarket instead, and after plugging in, we went off to explore.

As I have already said, Holmfirth is one of my favourite places, but even so, we did not wish to spend too much time here. We found the terrace that had been used as Norah Batty's home on a street called Scarfold just off Hollowgate and perhaps should not have been surprised to discover that it had now been turned into a holiday home, heavily promoting itself with its famous link. I do not blame the owners one bit, and I would probably do the same given a chance, had some crazy television producer turned up at my door and made my little semi-detached house famous overnight.

We wandered across town again and over the river to find another filming location from the series, this time the café. We could have used the Sainsburys store to get over the river, as for some reason, it was built spanning the River Holme, which seemed a bit odd, but instead, we used the bridge on Victoria Street.

We found the café immediately across the bridge and felt that we had no option other than to go in and sip some tea out of a saucer, as was the trademark of Bill Owen, the actor who played the rather rough but lovable character of Compo.

When the BBC first started filming the series, way back in 1970, the café had not in fact been a café at all but was being used as a storeroom by the ironmongers next door. Sometime after filming and smelling the sweet aroma of cash, the owners decide to fit it out exactly as it had looked in the TV series after hordes of fans started turning up who were clearly expecting to be able to pop in for a cup of tea and a slice of cake. They were clearly still doing well today, as the place was positively buzzing, but I suspect, like many other businesses of its type, it had been a struggle due to COVID-19 causing lockdown after lockdown, not only forcing businesses to close but compelling people to stay at home, save money, and stop snoring, or whatever the government's latest phrase was.

PAUL AMESS

Whenever I had been out with my walking friends, or on journeys such as this, we always make an effort to go into the local shops and pubs, and although my wife thinks this is just a ruse to stuff myself silly with pork pies and real ale, we really do try to support local businesses, something which is even more important in our post-pandemic world where people are desperately trying to get back on their feet, so this is something that I will earnestly continue to do until the day I die, and if I get fat as a result, then so be it, and I shall take one for the team

We had actually been a little bit longer than we had intended, and as a result, the car was more or less charged. We jumped back in but had not quite finished with this place yet. I explained to Rob that it was only a minute's drive to our next destination, the rather odd sounding Upperthong.

The drive was even shorter than I had expected, however, and as I pulled the car up outside St John's Church, wondering whether or not I should really leave the car on such a narrow lane and then deciding to be reckless and doing just that, we figured it would have been quicker to walk here from Nora Batty's house than to go back for the car.

We wandered to the back of the graveyard, which is where we found the grave of Bill Owen, one of the stars of the TV show filmed here, where we paid our respects. He actually had two gravestones for some reason, and although I had seen pictures of his grave that featured his trademark wellies that he was never seen out of, there was no sign of them today.

Immediately next to him was his co-star and good friend, Peter Sallis, and both graves were clearly very well kept. Sallis, who was also famous of course for the voice of Wallace in the wonderful *Wallace and Gromit* movies, had possibly one of the best quotations I had ever seen on a gravestone, and it simply read '*Have a cracking day!*', which not only made me smile from ear to ear but also made a cracking day much more likely, I had to say.

It was a history lesson next, I explained to Rob as we hopped back into the car to head towards Meltham. We parked next to the Pink Elephant, which was neither of the African or Asian types but was a café of the Persian type.

Meltham had nothing on Holmfirth, we unanimously decided, mere seconds after getting out of the car. We were not here for its looks anyway, but to find the former mills, which unfortunately all seemed to have disappeared over the last hundred years or so.

We had wanted to get a look at the area where a young lady called Dora Thewlis grew up but had to be content with a short walk around the town centre instead. Dora was born here in the late 1800s and became a keen member of the women's suffrage movement, which demanded equal voting rights for women.

Her parents were socialists and taught her how to read by the time she was 7 years old by using newspapers, even though they had another 6 children to bring up at the same time.

She joined the Women's Social and Political Union as soon as she could when she turned sixteen years old and was arrested the very same year when she broke into, of all things, the Houses of Parliament.

She was belittled by both the judge and the press, who labelled her the baby suffragette, and when the judge told her parents to take her home and sort her out, they replied that she was her own person, and anyway, they fully supported what she had done.

She achieved fame and notoriety when she was pictured wild-haired on the front page of the Daily Mirror the day after she was arrested. The picture shows a clearly defiant Thewlis being manhandled by some moustachioed bobbies who looked uncomfortable, to say the least.

Sadly, Thewlis never saw the suffrage that she had fought so hard for. She left England for Australia, never to return, dying there in 1976.

We drove to Marsden, where we had intended to stop, as the village was a popular filming location for many popular television programmes such as *The League of Gentlemen, Where the Heart Is,* and of course *Last of the Summer Wine,* but the place was positively heaving today, so we decided instead to avoid the crowds, and went to the Standedge Tunnel, or more accurately to the visitor centre.

There was plenty of free parking, and more importantly, toilets, and the place occupied a pleasant little site alongside a canal. Families enjoyed picnics while their young children ventured perilously close to the water's edge, with one young dad grabbing his toddler son mere seconds before he looked like he was going to go for a swim. Dogs ran amok around the place, and I am not sure if I am just getting old and cranky or if I have been locked up in my man cave at the bottom of the garden writing this stuff for too long, but I just didn't like it.

It wasn't the place as such, as the setting was lovely; it was just what was going on here that bothered me. Nonetheless, we were here now, so we wandered into the visitor centre to see what we could learn.

It was actually better inside, as there were fewer children, and we did, in fact, learn quite a lot. There are actually four tunnels, for instance, and the canal tunnel is the longest, highest and deepest in the United Kingdon, apparently. The original contractor backed out after various setbacks, and the cost of the venture threatened to spiral out of control, which all reminded me of the current attempt to build the new train line from London, HS2, and mused that some things never change.

The most interesting thing I learned, however, is that the phrase *to leg it*, meaning to run away, which I often used as a child when I may or may not have been about to run away from someone or somewhere after committing some mischief, comes from the canal world where young men, and it usually was men who were young it has to be said, would propel a canal boat through a tunnel by lying on their backs and pushing the thing along with their legs. It's amazing what you learn in a day, isn't it?

We had spent as much time here as we had either wanted or intended to, so after considering the menu in the small restaurant but deciding we were still full from the café in Holmfirth, we were once again on the road. Rob navigated as I threw the steering wheel this way and that, passing through villages such as Delph, Denshaw and Newhey, where nothing of any significance had ever happened, apparently.

We were, however, just a few miles north of Manchester. The drive down from the hills had given us some fine views towards the city, and while we were not venturing any further towards it on this trip, there are just a couple of things I feel compelled to say about it. Firstly, it absolutely always rains in Manchester. Every time I have ever been there, and every time I have thought about going, a quick check of the weather forecast always tells me that the chances of rain is usually somewhere around the hundred per cent mark, sometimes higher.

Secondly, it is, in fact, Manchester that probably gave us Sherlock Holmes, as Sir Arthur Conan Doyle more than likely partly based his fictitious character on a man named Jerome Caminada.

Caminada was born in the city in 1844, in perhaps the most crime-ridden district at that time, which was Deansgate. Growing up between brothels and slums, Caminada was perhaps influenced by his dismal surroundings, so he joined the local police force when he was just 24 years old.

The first police raids he led were not necessarily what you would call sophisticated, though, and would certainly not inspire a great detective such as Sherlock Holmes. For instance, in 1880, Caminada led a raid on a cross-dressing ball, basically a party, and arrested all those there for, well, nothing more than being in fancy dress basically.

After that, he became serious, though, and gained a formidable reputation by the mid-1880s, and he is said to have arrested over 1,000 serious criminals and closed hundreds of crime-ridden public houses throughout the city during his career. This all culminated in the arrest of Bob Horridge, literally Manchester's most wanted, who had become a notorious burglar and armed robber in the city over the last few years. Caminada had originally arrested Horridge for a relatively minor offence, but nonetheless, Horridge was given a long sentence of 7-years of hard labour. Upon his release, Horridge made it his mission in life to antagonise Caminada and became his real-life Professor Moriarty, culminating years later in a duel between the two, where Caminada managed to pull his revolver out a split second before Horridge. Caminada became famous, with his arrests regularly featuring in the national press. Criminals were even on first name terms with him, calling him Detective Jerome, though this was probably because they had problems saying his last name.

This period, then, is where the similarities with Sherlock Holmes are said to have begun. Caminada would often dress in disguise, for instance, so that he could surveil and catch his unwitting suspects, who were not used to such tactics. He also built up a huge number of informants and went to great efforts to keep them secret, even from his own bosses. Furthermore, his own superiors often failed to recognise Caminada when he was undercover. Caminada would often meet his contacts in the dark streets of Manchester in the middle of the night, again often in disguise, in hidden alleyways and at the back of a church, which all seems to be really cloak and dagger stuff, exactly like Holmes. Lastly, after he left the police force, Caminada became a private detective, so there you go.

Conan Doyle published his first book, which if you remember he wrote in Portsmouth where we started our journey north, in 1887, exactly at the height of Caminada's fame, and Sherlock Holmes became famous for adopting disguises and other clever tricks, which all sounds exactly like Jerome Caminada, it has to be said. Finally, Caminada died in 1914, and after the dignity of his career, his death was unfortunately not so, and he was hit by a bus. With his death, there also came the death of Sherlock Holmes, with the last story being set in 1914, a probable tribute to the great detective that had so inspired Sir Arthur Conan Doyle.

At Newhey, where we definitely left Manchester behind, we passed beneath the colossus that is the M62 motorway but did not stop to celebrate the fact. However, one thing that can be said for certain is that we were now well and truly in the north of England, and I reckoned we had been for quite some time. What brought me to this conclusion was the sight of an old man wearing a flat cap and walking a whippet, which is basically about as north of England as you get, it has to be said.

Our destination was Walsden, and we parked down by the canal near a rather vicious flock of geese. They had mistaken us for people who liked geese and who might actually feed them, and when they realised that there was no free food for them today, things soon became a bit nasty. One of them pecked at my trousers, and as I tried to scare it away, I accidentally stood on another one, but only just, no need to ring the animal rights people or anything, though this only made things worse.

Rob was stood some yards back from me, shouting out useful advice such as they are more scared of you than you are of them, and if you stand still, they will ignore you. Both statements proved to be absolute tosh, and I barely escaped with my life and figured I had probably lost several fingers and a couple of toes.

We wandered up the canal for a while, away from the demonic geese, and I explained to Robin the strange events that had happened to a policeman called Alan Godfrey, who had lived here for a while. Godfrey was a policeman and had been on duty on the night of 28th November 1980. It had been a normal shift, but when he went off to investigate a report of roaming cattle, he claims that he saw a white rotating light directly over him. Failing to radio this strange event in to his colleagues back at the police station as his radio would not work, the light then vanished, and Godfrey found himself suddenly transported 30 yards down the road and had lost several minutes.

Later on, through hypnotic regression, Godfrey recalled accounts of being taken aboard a strange craft after being blinded by a light that had been shone into his eyes before passing out. When he came back to consciousness, he discovered that he was then being examined by some small beings and also a larger man with a beard. This made national headlines, if only because Alan Godfrey was a well-respected police officer. While it is easy to dismiss such claims, three other police officers reported seeing something strange in the sky just a week before Alan Godfrey, and less than a month later, United States troops reported a UFO sighting at Rendlesham Forest, just outside RAF Woodbridge, which has since become one of the most famous UFO sightings in history.

There was nothing in the sky today, though, unless you included the clouds, that is, and as we headed to our next little treat, those very clouds decided to once again start to rain on us.

Bacup is not a place that I had ever been to. We were only here because this is the home to the Britannia Coconut Dancers, who are also affectionately known as The Nutters. If you form an image in your mind of Morris dancers crossed with Alice from Alice in Wonderland, with protective nuts to protect knees, waists and wrists, which are, of course, the coconuts, then that is the nutters.

However, the interesting thing about the nutters is that they blacken their faces, something that has gotten many a famous person into trouble recently. For the Nutters, however, the tradition is said to go back to the soot that would have done this to the miner's faces naturally and is nothing to do with black-face that causes such controversy elsewhere. Lastly, they are apparently quite famous, and the Sunday Times describes their dancing by saying that *nothing in the civilised world is quite as elementally bizarre and awkwardly compelling as the Coco-nutters of Bacup.* Well, it must be good if they say so. Additionally, I am glad to say that the nutters look set to continue their traditions for some time to come, and although they were not around today, I will be back next easter to see them in action, that is for certain.

It was time to charge the car again, although it still had plenty of juice. Still, I liked the fact that we had been charging it whenever it seemed to be approaching the halfway mark, as it meant that we never had to be concerned about the range.

Burnley looked promising, and with the watershed passing just to the east of the town, we would not have to go far out of our way. We found a rapid charger at the local Nissan dealership, and it was both available and working, so we went for a short walk to grab a coffee.

There is a lot that can be said about Burnley, such as it was important during the industrial revolution and it lost lots of men in the First World War, and this was also where Frank Whittle built his first successful jet engines once he had figured out how to do it.

Perhaps the most interesting story of the place, though, is that of Jabez Balfour, who was a businessman, politician and, get this, fraudster, being the MP for the town in the late 1800s. In 1892, he set up a series of companies, including a bank and a building society, though all of his companies failed spectacularly and in short order, suggesting foul play.

This was confirmed when Balfour immediately fled to Argentina, presumably with great wads of cash sticking out of his suitcases, where he fully intended to live out the rest of his life in absolute luxury and at the expense of others. Unfortunately for Balfour, one of Scotland Yard's most famous and efficient detectives was on his case, and that was Robert Froest.

The British Government had been engaging with the Argentine authorities to legally arrange Jabez Balfour's return to the United Kingdom, where he would face a fair trial before being convicted, of course.

Unfortunately, this proved to be far too complicated, so instead, Froest volunteered to pop down to the southern hemisphere, grab Balfour by the scruff of the neck, and drag him back home. By now, two years had passed, and it was some time in 1895 before this incident actually occurred, which can ultimately only be described as a state-sanctioned kidnapping. Ah, the good old days.

When Froest arrived in Argentia, then, he simply bundled Balfour onto a train and took him to a ship called The Tartar Prince, which then brought him home. Balfour was given his fair trial, found guilty of course, and sentenced to fourteen years hard labour, which he served in Portland Prison, Dorset.

Robert Froest continued his successful career, despite his hard to spell name and was later responsible for the largest mass arrest in British history, when in 1896, he arrested 26 officers and 399 crew on a ship called the S.S. Harlech Castle. This was because someone had decided that it would be a good idea to raid Johannesburg without any authority whatsoever, an event which was later said to be a cause of one of the bloodiest wars that England had ever fought, the Boer War, which started just a couple of years later in 1899.

Towards the end of his career, Froest was again in the news, as he was Chief Inspector Walter Dew's superior office during the Crippen case, and it would appear that Dew had certainly learned a thing or two from Froest. It was Dew that sailed to Canada to arrest the notorious murderer Dr Crippen, along with his mistress Ethel Le Neve. Froest was aware that Crippen had sailed to Canada but simply sent Dew on a faster ship to meet him there, where he made the arrest after initially impersonating the pilot of a ship.

With our coffee cups empty, we ventured back to the car and headed out of town to the northwest, in the direction of Colne, which was not too far away and seemed to be a part of Burnley, in that we did not notice any countryside between the two. We parked outside the library, for this is where we wanted to be, although we were definitely not after any books. There was supposed to be a life-sized bust here of a man called Wallace Hartley, and while you may think you do not know him, you will at least have heard of him, if only in popular culture. We could not, however, see any sign of a bust.

Wallace Hartley had been the bandleader on the Titanic and is famous for playing on while the ship sank into the cold, dark waters of the North Atlantic in the early hours of 15th April 1912, which was their attempt to help people keep calm, even in the face of almost certain death. Hartley did indeed ultimately die in the tragedy, but his body was recovered a couple of weeks later, after which he was brought home to be buried here in Colne, where it is said that forty thousand people lined the streets on the day of his funeral. Amazingly, his violin was handed in to the Salvation Army in Bridlington in 1939 and has recently sold for a little under a million pounds to a museum in Tennessee in the USA.

With no sign of the bust outside, though, I ventured into the library to ask them if they had perhaps lost it, and was told by a charming young woman that it was just down the road at the old library, and after thanking her, we wandered along to find it, and I'm glad we did. Not only did we find the bust, but there was a fantastic model of the Titanic next to it, which made my day.

It was not a long walk to the cemetery, although

we initially had to go back the way we had come, but once again, it was definitely worth it. Hartley's headstone must have been about ten feet tall and featured a violin carved just above the base, with the musical notes from the song *Nearer, my God, to thee*, which is the song the band are said to have played as the ship went down, and which is rather appropriate when you think about it

Hartley's legacy lives on, and his story has made it into every book and film ever written about the tragedy, being seen as such an important part of the events of that dreadful night. For their efforts to keep calm and carry on, one newspaper reported at the time on the actions of Hartley and his band, stating *the part played by the orchestra on board the Titanic in her last dreadful moments will rank among the noblest in the annals of heroism at sea.* I think anyone would find it hard to disagree with that statement.

It was now time to find somewhere to camp, which was easy, as we already knew of a campsite around here that came highly recommended by someone else, and it was Shay Gate Camping just to the northeast of the town.

Once again, we found ourselves on a working farm, but the field used for camping had a fantastic view over the valley to the south. I became a bit alarmed when I went to use the facilities, as a sign pointed into a horse trailer for the showers, and the toilets were in what looked like a portacabin, but both were spotlessly clean and appeared to be pretty new.

With our tents all set up, thankfully without encountering any rain, and with us both having scrubbed up pretty well, we decided to take the short walk to the local pub, which was the Emmott Arms. A footpath led from the campsite, more or less directly to the pub, which was a stroke of luck, as we were pretty hungry by this time of day.

Unfortunately, when we got to the pub and wandered in, it became clear that a reservation was required. One of the younger members of staff confirmed this, and it seemed that without a reservation, we were not eating, as the reservation only policy was a pretty strict one, he told us, with a serious face that suggested sour sweets. I asked him if there were perhaps any other pubs or takeaways within walking distance, or maybe a bit of roadkill that we could gnaw on, but he did not know of such things he promised us. When I asked him, then, if he was perhaps not from around here, I was surprised when he said that indeed he was, and he had lived here all of his life, at which point I not only gave up on the conversation but rather lost the will to live as well

From behind me, and out of nowhere, Robin shouted, and he did shout, that we did, in fact, have a reservation, and it was for 8.30pm. I knew this not to be so, so when the young man went off to find us a table, Rob told me that he had just gone online and booked one. What a good idea, I thought to myself, though I gave Rob none of the satisfaction of knowing my thoughts on this, lest he gets ideas above his station.

A chilli beef and a roast chicken later, where once again Rob's food had looked far superior to mine, we enjoyed a single solitary pint before heading back to the campsite, determined to avoid any dark and splashy adventures. The sky had cleared, and the stars were twinkling, and it occurred to me that we were rapidly losing the summer, and the nights were certainly drawing in all around us.

I remembered my commitment to sit and enjoy the starry nights, and invited Rob to join me, and seeing as this was possibly our last night out like this, we decided to celebrate with a further bottle of beer which would hopefully help us enjoy a perfect night of sleep in a couple of hours' time.

We sat in our chairs enjoying nature's display and saw a handful of shooting stars as well as several satellites pass over us, although we saw no aliens or UFOs unless, of course, our minds had been wiped.

We talked about how far we had come and how we had been to so many places in a matter of days, with us each choosing our highlights from each day that we had travelled. I had particularly enjoyed Boscobel House and Lud's Church, and Rob said that his favourite places had been the Rollright Stones, the gatehouse in Ashby St Ledgers where the gunpowder plot had been planned, and our wander around Winchester, which had definitely been a highlight for me too, but which now seemed to be so far away and so long ago.

We enjoyed nature's spectacle, and by the time we decided to turn in, our eyes had adjusted to the dark conditions fully, which allowed us to see a night sky so full of stars that it was hard to make out what was what.

That night I dreamed of nothing and had one of the best nights of sleep I can ever recall getting in a tent.

THE DASH FOR
THE BORDER

Dawn broke to a vivid red sky on what was probably going to be our last day on the road, and I wondered if the old saying about it being a shepherd's warning would mean bad weather later on. There was no sign of anything untoward, and as Rob and I quietly cooked our breakfast and made a cup of coffee, we noticed only a couple of other campers stirring at such an early hour.

Breakfast today was porridge oats, sweetened by treacle, a favourite of Rob's, and it was quickly becoming a favourite of mine.

We chatted quietly over the stove in hushed tones, and we both agreed that we had to go for it today and must therefore make it to the Scottish border by this evening as we had to head straight home after that. Other commitments beckoned us, and I, for one, was going to miss our daily routine, which had become charging and travelling, and then eat, sleep and repeat.

We drove out of the campsite, grateful for the silent electric motor of the car as it was still only a little past 5am, and we followed the farm track back to the road and headed for Foulridge, where there was a nice canal and tunnel.

We parked in the car park of a pub called The Wharf, which was quite fittingly on the wharf next to the canal, and walked back down to find the tunnel that took the canal underground towards Burnley. This only took us a minute, so we sat for a while, enjoying the peace and tranquillity all around us. This stretch was actually a part of the Leeds to Liverpool Canal, and the tunnel is also known as the Mile Tunnel, although it is a hundred yards or so short of that title, really.

There should not, in fact, be a tunnel here at all, but instead, there should have been a series of locks. Thanks, however, to our American cousins and their dreams for independence, the Revolutionary War caused the project to be put on hold for a few years, which was then scaled back for reasons of cost. One of the results of this is that most of the tunnel was actually created using the cut and cover method, where the hill above was carted away bit by bit, which then allowed the structure of the tunnel to be put in place, after which the hill was dragged back to cover the lot, thereby magically creating a tunnel where none existed before. As I sat pondering this effort, which seemed like a lot of work, it has to be said, I did wonder if it would have just been easier to build some locks, but there you go.

While all this historical stuff is interesting, of course, the real reason we are here is because of a silly cow. And before anyone gets offended, I mean an actual animal, though clearly a rather stupid one at that.

Legend has it that on 24th September 1912, Buttercup, as the rather brainless bovine was known, fell into the canal close to Blue Slate Farm, which is at the other side of the big hill that sat before us today and was where she lived with her owner Robin Brown. Unable to extract herself from this splashy ordeal, she instead swam through the entire length of the tunnel and emerged more or less exactly where we now sat, somewhat worse for wear but at least still alive.

Locals then dragged her out, and seeing her distressed condition, did what any concerned neighbour would do in such circumstances and took Buttercup straight to the pub, reviving her with the best part of a bottle of brandy. There is certainly some substance to this rather tall tale, and a photo of the unlucky beast still exists to this day, with the locals being very proud of the story indeed.

While we are talking about cows, it is also worth pointing out that they can be pretty dangerous. I do a lot of country walking and have had several what I would call spicy encounters with the beasts over the years. In fact, statistically speaking, cows are more dangerous than sharks, so don't say you haven't been warned.

We were soon rolling again, however, as time waits for no man, this time heading towards Barnoldswick, distinctive for being the highest point of the Leeds to Liverpool Canal but also for being where the longest ever strike occurred in the UK, when workers at the Silentnight factory threw their tools down in 1985 and refused to make any more beds until 1987.

The factory is still there, so we popped in to see if we could use their charger, but we knew the answer before the car even stopped. The security was nothing compared to what we had seen at the Dyson factory, but a 20-foot fence, a raised barrier and security cameras all told us we had no chance, so I swung the car around, and we carried on our way.

Our next stop was Hellifield, where we discovered we really had arrived in the Yorkshire Dales, as dry stone walls were everywhere, which were all very pretty and nice, but did not charge electric cars up very well, or at all come to think of it. Robin had checked the app, which had been difficult as the phone signal was not very good out here in the wilds, but eventually, we figured that the next viable charger was at Horton-in-Ribblesdale, still quite some way off.

We had not done many miles so far today, but the terrain and the constant up and downhill driving was killing the battery quicker than we had seen on any other part of this journey, so we felt compelled to stick to our route as closely as we could, and to drive as slowly as possible when it was safe to do so.

We didn't stop in Hellifield, then, not that there was much to see by the looks of it, and similarly, we drove straight through Long Preston, which certainly lived up to the first part of its name.

As we made our way towards Settle, we felt as if we were in familiar territory, having been up here recently to walk the Yorkshire Three Peaks. Rob has probably done this walk around a dozen times, though it was only my second time doing it and was probably my last.

It is not that I didn't enjoy it; in fact, I really did, but it's just that I would rather do something different and see somewhere new rather than see the same things over and over again.

The walk takes in the three hills known as Pen-y-Ghent, Whernside and Ingleborough, with considerable distances to cover between the peaks, and comes in at around the same distance as what running a marathon would be if we were ever silly enough to do one, which we are not. It is said that you should aim to do the walk in less than twelve hours, but this is entirely up to you, and when I last did it, I certainly did not rush. Personally speaking, the last climb was the hardest for me, as the ascent of Ingleborough Hill involves something akin to a rock scramble, and considering I had already been walking for several hours and was pretty exhausted at this point, it nearly finished me off.

If you have never been to Settle, I can tell you that it is a lovely little place, so we decided to stop for a coffee. There is a famous café here called The Naked Man, but as we pulled up and parked in the market square, I was reminded that its full name is Ye Olde Naked Man. While we were there, the town was in the middle of its traditional flower pot season, where villagers and shopkeepers build what look like scarecrows out of flower pots and decorate them in various ways. The effort this year was as good as any I could remember, with my favourite being a giraffe up towards the post office, though I did nearly manage to get myself run over when I stepped into the road to better frame my picture, which at least made Rob laugh a little.

Our next stop would be Horton-in-Ribblesdale, and after spending less than an hour in Settle, we were once again on our way but made an impromptu stop at a mill, where I can say that I certainly gave the brakes on the old Leaf a good test as we drove past it.

We had to stop, really, as the mill was called The Watershed Mill, and was the first mention of the watershed that we had come across on this journey, so we dumped the car in the car park and went to find the story of this place.

Unfortunately, the two people I spoke to inside had no idea what the name meant and sort of looked at me as if I was something the cat had just dragged in. Undaunted, we had a good look around, and although we did not find a mill as such, we did find lots of trinkets and other stuff that we didn't need, or maybe perhaps just didn't know we needed yet.

There was, however, a nice little café, and even though we had just stopped in Settle for one, we decided to have another one here, because this one would be accompanied by a large fresh scone, complete with jam and cream.

Robin had to spoil it, though, as when his arrived, he put the cream on first and then the jam, which is obviously the wrong way around, but when I told him of his error, he just became defensive and made out as if I was the crazy person.

The lady who brought the scones turned out to be called Emma and was very friendly and helpful. She told us that the place started off as a weaving mill but later on was used to make paper, before lying unused for several years, after which it became a small shopping outlet. We told her that we were driving up the watershed and explained that was why we had stopped, and she then took great delight in telling us that the river that ran just behind the mill, the River Ribble, has its source nearby, just near the famous Ribblehead Viaduct, hence the name of the mill. Finally, we had met someone who knew at least something about the watershed, we thought, as it had until then appeared that this is something nobody had ever thought about, but then why would they?

We finished off our scones, and with that feeling you get when you have eaten such things that tells you your face around your mouth is still covered in food, we hit the road once again, this time to go and find that charger in Horton-in-Ribblesdale.

On the way, though, we did stop once more, this time in the tiny hamlet of Stainforth. We parked outside a pub called the Craven Heifer, which I will tell you about later, as we were going to have a walk down to one of the waterfalls in the area. Stainforth Falls is possibly the best known, but we had already been there on previous walks, so this time we were heading for Catrigg Falls, where neither of us had ever been but which was only a short walk to the east.

We followed a small track out of the village called Goat Scar Lane, which was little more than a path bounded by dry stone walls on both sides. A brisk 20-minute walk took us to the end of the lane, and as we knew we had to turn off when the dry stone walls ended, we headed left and into some trees. We began to hear the sound of the waterfall as we neared the spot, and as we came to the beck and looked right, Catrigg Falls was suddenly before us in all its glory.

The waterfall is pretty dramatic and marks the spot where water cascades down a steep drop and through a narrow chasm into a lovely pool below. If we had been here in the searing heat of a few days ago, I think we would both have been in that pool without hesitation, but with today's lower temperatures, the temptation seemed to have vanished.

Interestingly, this spot was perhaps the favourite place in Yorkshire of renowned classical composer Edward Elgar, and he is said to have drawn much inspiration from the beauty of the Yorkshire Dales for his most famous works, *Pomp and Circumstance* and the *Enigma Variations*.

When I first found this out, it meant nothing to me, but for *Pomp and Circumstance*, think Land of Hope and Glory instead, and it is the exact same thing but going by a different name and without the lyrics. The lyrics were added by A.C. Benson in 1901, which made it a favourite of Queen Victoria, though this was just before she died. When I say just before Queen Victoria died, I do not mean immediately before, I should point out, so don't go thinking that this song killed the longest-reigning monarch we have ever had, which would be just silly. Anyway, Victoria liked it a lot, and it quickly became associated with patriotism.

It was even proposed as a national anthem for England, which is distinctly different to the national anthem for the UK as a whole, of course, which is and will forever be God Save the Queen. Other proposals included *Jerusalem*, and rather cheekily I thought, *Heaven Knows I'm Miserable Now*, by *The Smiths,* but hell, if you can't laugh at yourself, what can you laugh at? I am also somewhat ashamed to add that the last suggestion came from listeners of the local and rather anachronistic BBC radio station where I live, which is BBC Humberside, with Humberside itself ceasing to exist many years ago, and the area is now known simply as East Yorkshire. Jerusalem, by the way, remained the favourite, but the whole thing never came to be, so England remains anthem-less, so to speak.

As we sat resting and looking at the beautiful waterfall, Robin, using the miracle of technology that almost all of us now carry around with us, managed to download Land of Hope and Glory, and we sat there, humbled, listening to it in one of the very places that brought the song to life. I am not ashamed to say that I felt chills in my body and all of my hairs stood on end.

We wandered back down the lane to Stainforth with not a soul in sight and soon found ourselves back at the car, and of course, the pub, the Craven Heifer, named after a famous cow of many moons ago. Bred by a man of the cloth, the Reverend William Carr, he deliberately fattened her up when he realised what he had in his possession, which was the biggest cow anyone had ever seen, and took her on a nationwide tour in 1812, charging people who wished to come and view this beastly bovine a shilling each, which was a princely sum a couple of hundred years ago.

The cow was bred at Bolton Abbey and was taken down to Smithfield Market in London, but the Reverend stopped at many pubs on the way to show his animal, many of which changed their name to the Craven Heifer in tribute to the visit. It is possible, then, that this is exactly how this pub got its name, but as it is closed as we stand outside it, there is no way for me to check.

It was just a couple of miles to Horton-in-Ribblesdale, which looked very familiar to us. We knew this place well, having stayed at a campsite in the village many times, and soon found the car park where the charger was located. Not surprisingly, there were no electric cars plugged into it, being out in the middle of nowhere as we were and at a relatively early hour, but there was an ordinary car parked in one of the bays. Furthermore, it had parked in such a manner that left the next bay unusable, being over the lines of the bay and effectively blocking both bays off.

There is a name for this, when normal cars, and I use the term normal to mean petrol and diesel ones, block off a charger, and the bay is said to be iced. This basically means that a vehicle with an internal combustion engine (i.c.e.) has parked where it shouldn't.

I suspected I knew why, and sure enough, I found a blue disabled badge in the front window of the offending vehicle. I had seen this several times before, and it happens when incredibly old and probably blind people mistake a bay for electric cars with a bay for disabled drivers. I can only assume that they see the paint of the tarmac and are not paying enough attention to see what it actually is, and I also wonder how such people manage to arrive at their destinations alive.

Luckily, the charging cable that we have is long enough for such eventualities. I had learned from the experiences of my cousin, who bought a slightly shorter lead to save a few pounds, that it was simply not worth it, so I had gone for a longer cable that was some 5-metres long.

Still, the Leaf looked to be parked very badly indeed, so I put a short note in the window that would hopefully explain to any passing traffic warden that once again, no, I was not Stevie Wonder but was just trying to charge my car so I would not have to spend the rest of my life out here in the wilderness.

There is not a lot to be found in Horton-in-Ribblesdale, certainly no traffic wardens hopefully, but it is a centre for walking and caving in the many beautiful hills and valleys that surround the place, which makes it very popular.

We wandered down to the church and sat for a while looking at the walkers setting off on the three-peaks challenge, then had a walk into the campsite where we had stayed previously, just to say hello to the owners, really.

They were in, and we had a little chat, but I don't think they recognised us, but then they do get hundreds of people going through each week, so this is not surprising, really. They are very nice people and have built a huge tent at the edge of the campsite where they keep an eye on things, and to be honest, I suspect they actually live in that tent.

In pre-pandemic days, when you could actually go inside places without people having panic attacks or quickly putting on hazmat suits, I had been in there and had found a veritable treasure trove of books, trinkets and more, as well as chairs and sofas, a wood-burning stove, and even a piano. I remembered falling to sleep on a night while listening to them all having a sing-song, which was actually fantastic, and I remember feeling jealous of their lifestyle, as they were obviously very happy.

We continued our little wander around the village, and although I tried to check the app on my phone, which would show me how much the car was charged, I had no signal, so I could not do so. After what we reckoned had been more than an hour, though, we wandered back to the car and found that the flashing lights on the dashboard indicated that the car was almost fully charged, so we prepared to depart.

At this moment, another electric car arrived, a Volkswagen, and the driver did not look happy about the other bay being occupied by a regular car. She was about to drive away, so I flagged her down and told her that we were leaving, making her smile. As we talked about the next nearest charging options to the north, which she said was in Hawes but was a slow one, she also told me that we had missed one in Stainforth, where we could have topped up the car while we were walking, which was annoying. It had not been on the app, apparently because it was new.

As I unplugged the leaf, two elderly people arrived to claim the car that had been blocking the other charging bay. An elderly man was pushing an equally elderly lady in a wheelchair, and as I said good morning to them, I explained to them that where they had been parking was not a disabled bay at all. He looked at me for a minute and simply told me that they had been for a nice walk and had enjoyed an ice cream near the bridge, so I just smiled and wished them well and did not have the heart to explain again.

I pulled out of the space and into another one so that the Volkswagen driver could plug her car in, then checked the map to see where we would be going. We decided to head for Kirkby Stephen, where a rapid charger would enable us to continue our journey but would then have to deviate slightly off route for another rapid charge at Penrith. After this, chargers were slow and well-spaced out, so we would have to be careful to plan our route unless we wanted to run out of charge in the middle of the countryside and probably in an area with no phone signal, which would be a complete disaster.

We left Horton-in-Ribblesdale behind, heading north along a beautiful valley, with the road bounded on either side by a continuous dry-stone wall. This was good, as there were thousands of sheep on either side of us, apparently roaming free around the national park.

We soon got our first glimpse of the Ribblehead Viaduct and simply had to stop to admire it as soon as we had found the car park. This was a popular spot today, with countless cars parked around the area and with tiny dots of walkers disappearing up the hills in every direction you looked.

A train passed over the viaduct as we stood admiring it from below, but rather than a nice old steam train, this one was a lot more modern. We were only out of the car for a few minutes, and with nothing else to see, we decided to move on.

Time was also running out. A considerable part of the day had passed, and we had not made as much progress as we had wished, and as we both had commitments tomorrow, we now had to make some difficult decisions about our next few stops.

For this reason, we did not stop in Hawes, which was a shame, as we had wanted to see one of the most miserable shopkeepers in the country if you believed what you read in the press. The bookshop in the town had been owned by a man called Steve Bloom, who had introduced a policy of charging people 50-pence just to come into his shop even before they had bought anything, a sum I would have happily paid to have a chat with a fellow grumpy old man.

Instead, we went straight to Buttertubs Pass, which was beautiful, though we only got out of the car for a quick photo opportunity and to enjoy the striking views down into the valley ahead of us. The car was once again telling us that we might not make it to our destination, though we expected it to change its mind when we started driving down the other side of the large mountain we had just come up, and indeed it did.

We drove straight through Keld as well, although once again we had been here many times and were quite familiar with this beautiful little village along with its waterfalls, and we even forced ourselves to ignore the sign that pointed up into the hills and to the Tan Hill Inn, England's highest pub. We went instead straight on to Kirkby Stephen, where we were grateful to find that the charger was both working and available. Because this was a rapid charger, we did not have to mill about for long, although there is a lot to see in this little town, with its fine church dubbed the Cathedral of the Dales along with many fantastic walks in the local area.

We admired Brough Castle through the windows as we sailed past, and similarly did not stop at Appleby-in-Westmoreland, famous for its horse fair, but instead drove straight through to Penrith, where we found the next rapid charger was also available and in good working order, and figured that we had been lucky that this was so.

We then had to take another look at the map, as the last part of our journey just did not look possible for us, at least not in this car. With around fifty miles to go before the Scottish border, but with only one slow charger in between here and there, which was out of order according to the app we were using, we had a difficult choice to make. Did we risk it and hope to make it in one go, or should we go from here to Carlisle, grab another rapid charge, and then head for the border.

Both of us were undecided, as although it would be fun to give it a go, it just seemed irresponsible, yet to go to Carlisle seemed a little like giving up, which meant there was only one thing left to do – we would let the queen decide.

I took out a coin and told Robin that if it was heads, we were going for it, and we were going to Carlisle if it was tails. I waited for him to nod his head in agreement and then tossed the coin, giving it the best spin I could manage.

It hung in the air for what seemed like an eternity, and while it went round and round, it did not seem to fall, at least not for a second.

When it finally hit the ground, it was still spinning, and it was impossible to tell which way this would go. I looked at Rob, who looked back at me, and then we both gazed at the coin, transfixed as we were with its painfully slow journey.

Finally, it began to lose momentum, and we slowly began to make out the heads and tails sides alternating before us in what was a giddy dance. As it slowed and slowed, we wondered which way it would go until the coin stopped, was motionless for a second on its side, and then it fell.

It was heads, and I remarked to Robin that we were going across country, with no chargers, probably no phone signal, and that if I were to die in the wilderness, he should tell my family I loved them. After making a last will and testament and buying enough provisions to keep us going for several winters, we unplugged the car, said goodbye to civilization, and with that, we were off.

We first headed for Melmerby, and although we had decided to curtail most of our stops on this last section of our journey, this was one that we could simply not cross off the list. For it is near Melmerby that the Long Meg stone circle can be found, full name Long Meg and her Daughters, although technically Long Meg is the name of the single standing stone just outside the circle to the south, with the stones of the stone circle being the daughters.

Although the circle was a mile or so off the main road, which used up valuable range, it was well worth the visit, although I did wonder when we pulled up which moron had built a track straight through the ancient monument and had been too lazy to take it 30-feet to the east instead.

We had the place to ourselves, walked around the perimeter, took a couple of photos, and then just stood and enjoyed the silence that was all around us. I had read that there are around a thousand stone circles in the UK, so to give you a rough idea of how good this one was, it is probably the best one after Stonehenge, which is saying something. Don't think you have to take my humble word on this. It was none other than William Wordsworth himself, one-time poet laureate, that said of this place *next to Stonehenge it is beyond dispute the most notable relic that this or probably any other country contains,* so there you go, although I guess he had never been to Egypt or Peru, or a lot of other places come to think of it.

The name comes from a legend surrounding the circle and tells the story of a witch called Long Meg who, along with her daughters, refused to observe the sabbath. They dance wildly on the moors, a crime for which the punishment meant they were turned to stone, which is supposedly how the stone circle came to be. And the magic that is said to have created it continues to this day, with it being said that it is impossible to count the same number of stones twice, and if you do, the magic is broken. There are sixty-nine of them, by the way. I know this for sure as I counted them twice.

We only stayed long enough as was necessary, and with Robin navigating, I told him once again to get his left and right, well, right, as otherwise we would run out of fuel and have to live off the land for the rest of our lives.

We headed for Brampton, which meant that we would miss out on Slaggyford. While there had been nothing, in particular, to draw us there, I was disappointed purely and simply because it was such an amusing name. I had wanted a picture of us at the sign with the village's name on, which I would file away with the one I took of us in Willey.

Brampton was nice enough, and as we navigated the streets looking for the car park with the charger, we were both on edge, wondering if it would work, what with it being the last one in the country, of course. When we first saw the charger, everything looked good, so we pulled in and got out. However, when we looked at the information sticker on the charger, it seemed that we would have to subscribe as a monthly customer to get it working, which would cost £30. I checked this once, then just like Santa, I checked this twice, and it seemed preposterous that I would have to pay so much just for a single charge.

Looking at the map and the range left on the car, I suggested we forget about charging here and head for the rapid charger at the border. The road did not look too hilly, and there certainly wouldn't be a lot of traffic on the road, so we could probably drive really slowly, which would maximise our range, so perhaps quite irresponsibly, we drove out of Brampton without topping up the charge, but at least I was £30 richer. The next charger, at the Pentonbridge Inn, was only around 13 miles away, and according to the car, we had 19, so as the sun started to set around us, we headed off into the borderlands with more than just a hint of apprehension. In retrospect, we were just wondering where exactly we would run out of fuel, and not if, as we were both certain that our recklessness was going to catch up with us very soon.

The road was a nice wide one, which was a surprise and was bounded by hedges on either side but which still allowed us to see the beautiful countryside we were passing through. There were a few farms and cottages along the way, which reassured me that this area was not the wilderness I had thought it would be, and which meant that at least there would be someone to beg for electricity if we really did run out.

A couple more villages passed us by, with the last one being Boltonfellend, and it was shortly after this when the computer in the leaf gave us that ominous warning that we might not have enough range to make it to our destination. This was a surprise, as we had been running at a steady two- or three-miles more range than what we needed, and the actual range of the car had seemed to just lose a few miles completely inexplicably.

Around five miles short of the pub, we received yet another warning, this one stating that we had an extremely low battery charge and that we should find a charger immediately, which was easier said than done in the middle of nowhere.

Luckily, the roads were more or less flat, and as Rob directed us first right and then left, I thought to myself that he had finally nailed which was which. This was also when the range indicator went to zero, and we were once again waiting for that dreaded tortoise to appear. Of course, when it did, it would mean that we had exactly one mile left in the car, which would also be when we should start praying, I suggested to Rob.

The tortoise appeared at the last junction before the pub, and only because I had to reluctantly brake, so we did not get hit by the large truck that came thundering past as we approached the crossroads. However, I did not notice any change in speed, as I had already slowed right down to conserve whatever little juice we had left in the old leaf.

Finally, in the distance, we saw what we thought was the pub and gritted our teeth as we coasted slowly towards it, much to the annoyance of the boy racer that had appeared from behind out of nowhere and seemed to be stuck to my bumper. At seven minutes past ten, and in almost complete darkness, we finally pulled into the car park of the pub and parked next to the charger, which is when we both realised we had been holding our breath for the last couple of minutes.

Unfortunately, this charger was not a rapid one after all, although to be honest, we were just grateful that it worked at all. I had mistakenly earlier thought this was a fast charger, a mistake which we now realised would mean that we might be here for quite some time.

We went into the pub and grabbed a drink, as, after all, we certainly deserved one. Unfortunately, though, we only had a coke as we now figured we would be driving through the night, or at least we would once the car had charged in three or four hours.

As we sat in the pub, incidentally listening to one of the finest fiddle players I had ever heard, we checked the app to see where we were and where we would be going next, if anywhere, and we discovered that there was, in fact, a rapid charger just up the road and that it was working earlier that day, according to the app. This meant we would not have to wait here for so long after all, but just long enough to get us the nine miles to the next charger, so we sat back with a big grin on our faces and enjoyed the entertainment that we had been so lucky to stumble across.

An hour later, and as the pub prepared to close, we checked the car and discovered we had over 20 miles of range, which was more than enough to get us to Newcastleton and a fast charge. We got there just before midnight, which of course meant that the charger was not in use, after which we plotted a route that would lead us south and home, exclusively with rapid chargers along the way. Kielder was next, followed by Hexham, Durham, Ripon, York, and then finally Hull. We were home. We had made it, and we had covered over 1,000 miles.

CONCLUSION

When we got home, and after chatting on the way back, both Rob and I had incredibly mixed feelings about our little road trip. Yes, technically, we had made it, but it had not been the experience we had expected, and this was for various reasons.

We had anticipated the odd problem with a charger along the way, but the whole variety of problems had been more than expected. We had arrived at chargers to find them already occupied by other electric vehicles, which was fine as we knew we must wait our turn but also to find other vehicles blocking them, which is really not fine.

Chargers had also been faulty on occasions or had appeared to be working but had simply failed to charge the car. One charger, in particular, got my attention, as it deducted £150 from my bank account after I tried to get it working multiple times, only for it to deliver electricity worth a paltry eleven pence to the car before disconnecting. I got the money back eventually, but that was little consolation when I found my available balance was almost zero, and I could not withdraw cash for a couple of days.

To put this into perspective, when was the last time you pulled up at a petrol station and wondered whether or not there would be a pump available for you? Or would the pump be faulty, or even if there would be an abandoned car there which would mean you could not get near the pump and therefore could not fill up?

These things obviously never happen, except in the fuel crisis of 2021, of course, that saw panic buying create a self-fulfilling prophecy of temporary fuel shortages. We generally don't give theses ideas a second thought, but these problems will all have to be solved well before we have twenty million electric cars on the road. Otherwise, we may see instances of charge-rage, similar, of course, to road-rage. This problem will hopefully solve itself, though, as more chargers become available, and cars evolve larger or more efficient batteries and do therefore not have to charge up as often.

At the time of this trip, however, the sheer lack of chargers in certain areas was a particular problem, though this can only improve with time, and even in areas where there does seem to be a relatively high number of chargers, the fact that more and more cars are being sold every day will soon make charger scarcity a real issue if charger installations do not keep pace with sales.

Range anxiety fits into this as well, and there were

many times when we were wondering whether or not we would make it to our destination, although we only ever failed to do so on one occasion, which was down to human error and quite frankly could have happened in a car fuelled by petrol or diesel. Still, this is obviously a lot more unlikely given the longer range of these cars.

Another issue is the possible theft of charging cables, so I always used a physical lock on mine. However, newer cars are increasingly being made with the ability to lock the cable in place while charging, although it is only a matter of time until thieves figure out a way to get around any such measures. With a new, good quality cable costing more than one hundred pounds, it would not only spoil your day if someone stole yours, but it would also mean that you may be unable to continue your journey if you are unable to charge your car.

On a positive note, the journey had been some-what enjoyable, if not a little tiring, although I fully appreciate that we were travelling in a style that was trying to prove a point, in that was it or was it not possible to do this type of road trip in an old electric car, and that most people would not choose to travel as we did.

What is more, the journey had proven to be incred-ibly cost-effective. We had driven just over a thou-sand miles yet had spent just £25.33 on electricity to charge the car, as we had been able to use the slower, free chargers for much of the time. At current prices, and considering the free charging, this is the equivalent of getting around 250 miles per gallon in our tired old Leaf, which is reason enough to get one in itself. If I had done this trip in my wife's car, which gets around 50 miles per gallon, this trip would have cost approximately five times what we had paid out over the last few days.

A downside to this type of journey, though, was the time taken to charge the car. For every hour we drove, we would have to charge for two hours if we were at a slow charger, which is great when you can go for a wander around wherever you happen to be, such as when we were in places like Winchester but is not so great when you just want to charge and get going again. This was often the case when no rapid charger was available in an area and is why we spent many hours sat in supermarket car parks, or more often than not, going into those supermarkets and spending lots of money. However, most modern electric cars do charge much quicker than our ageing Leaf, so this should become less of a problem as time goes by.

Our final verdict then is as follows. Would we consider our trip to have been a success? Yes, certainly, but there are things we could have done better. For instance, as things stand now, a certain level of planning is required if you intend to drive long distances in an electric car, no matter how large the battery may currently be. This is because you simply cannot guarantee that there will be a charger wherever you are going. Or if there is one, it may already be occupied or may not work. So, you need a backup plan, or better still, a breakdown membership.

And would I recommend an electric car to anyone considering getting one? Again, yes, absolutely. No matter which one you choose, and this even includes our ageing Leaf, the vast majority of your journeys will be short ones, and electric cars are ideal for this. They are cheaper to run, although they currently cost more to buy, but over the lifetime of the vehicle this will balance out in favour of electric over petrol or diesel any day. And of course, they are also much better for the environment, and whether we currently want one or not, there will come a time when we have no choice.

As for the journey itself, we visited some fantastic and beautiful places and found the sources of some of our most famous rivers. We obviously could not stick to the watershed exactly, and in fact, had to deviate considerable distances several times to charge, but we kept the spirit of the trip alive, though we did not manage to drive up the middle of England without crossing a bridge.

I stand by my statement that you could draw a line across any part of our beautiful little island, and no matter where you ended up, you would be surrounded by amazing beauty and equally amazing history. And it's also amazing how various places are somehow linked one way or another, often in quite obscure ways, such as links to Sherlock Holmes or the civil war.

We had also managed to have quite a lot of fun on this journey, too, despite falling into rivers and running out of battery charge and getting lost late at night and having to sleep in a farmer's field. And of course, we had met some incredibly nice people who had helped us out in one way or another, either by telling us little snippets about where they lived or by helping us get a puncture fixed, which I never did tell Rob about, by the way.

So, if you are thinking about taking the leap to electric, then I can only give you one bit of advice, do it, and do it now.

BOOKS BY THIS AUTHOR

54 Degrees North

Rambling On: Lost On The Cleveland Way

Coast To Coast: Finding Wainwright's England

Hadrian's Wall Path: A Walk Through History

A Walk On The Wild Side: The Yorkshire Wolds Way

Printed in Great Britain
by Amazon

42784320R00158